Yes, Prime Minister

Antony Jay has enjoyed a distinguished career as writer, broadcaster and producer. He was founder and editor of the BBC's legendary *Tonight* programme and is editor of *The Oxford Dictionary of Political Quotations*, and author of *Elizabeth R* and two documentaries on the Royal Family. He is a Commander of the Royal Victorian Order.

Jonathan Lynn's prolific career spans more than four decades as a director, screenwriter, producer and actor in films, television and theatre, as well as best-selling author and novelist. His many movies include *Nuns on the Run* (which he also wrote), *My Cousin Vinny*, *The Whole Nine Yards* and *Wild Target*.

Jonathan Lynn and Antony Jay's BAFTA award-winning political comedy *Yes, Minister* first aired on BBC2 in 1980 and ran until 1984. The sequel, *Yes, Prime Minister*, ran from 1986 until 1988. The programmes have been seen in 84 countries, and both series are now available on BBC DVD. They won a Special Award from the Campaign for Freedom of Information, and numerous other awards.

Lynn and Jay also wrote three novels, *The Complete Yes, Minister* and *Yes, Prime Minster*, Volumes 1 and 2 (in paperback combined as *The Complete Yes Prime Minister*) which cumulatively sold more than a million copies in hardback, were on the British top-ten bestseller list for three years and have been translated into numerous languages.

ANTONY JAY
and
JONATHAN LYNN

Yes, Prime Minister

faber and faber

First published in 2010
by Faber and Faber Limited
74–77 Great Russell Street, London WC1B 3DA

Typeset by Country Setting, Kingsdown, Kent CT14 8ES
Printed in England by CPI Bookmarque, Croydon, Surrey

A CIP record for this book
is available from the British Library

ISBN 978-0-571-26070-6

2 4 6 8 10 9 7 5 3 1

Acknowledgements

Thank you to Bernard Donoughue
for his help and friendship over thirty years
of *Yes Minister* and *Yes Prime Minister*.

Thank you also to Marcia Falkender
for so much help and information throughout
the writing of the television series.

We also thank numerous other people
who would rather not be identified.

AJ, JL

Yes, Prime Minister, the play, was first presented on 13 May 2010 at Chichester Festival Theatre. The cast, in order of appearance, was as follows:

Sir Humphrey Appleby Henry Goodman
Bernard Woolley Jonathan Slinger
Jim Hacker David Haig
Claire Sutton Emily Joyce
Kumranistan Ambassador Sam Dastor
Jeremy Burnham William Chubb
Simon Chester Tim Wallers

Director Jonathan Lynn
Designer Simon Higlett
Lighting Designer Tim Mitchell
Casting Director Gabrielle Dawes

Characters

Sir Humphrey Appleby
Cabinet Secretary

Bernard Woolley
Principal Private Secretary
to the Prime Minister

Jim Hacker
Prime Minister

Claire Sutton
Special Policy Adviser

The Kumranistan Ambassador

Jeremy Burnham
Director-General of the BBC

Robin Simpson
BBC press officer
(voice only)

Simon Chester
BBC presenter

Driver, Cameramen

YES, PRIME MINISTER

The action takes place in the Prime Minister's study at Chequers, his official country residence.

Autumn. Friday afternoon to Sunday morning.

Act One

SCENE ONE

Late afternoon on an autumn Friday.

Jim's study, a comfortably furnished panelled room in Chequers, an English country mansion. It has a desk, a seating area, double doors (stage right), a smaller door (left) and big windows upstage centre.

Sir Humphrey Appleby and Bernard Woolley are waiting. Humphrey is standing, Bernard is sitting.

Newsreader (*on TV*) And now, weather. Severe thunderstorms are forecast . . .

Humphrey switches off the TV. Bernard puts down the Evening Standard.

Bernard It's awful, isn't it?

Humphrey What is awful, Bernard?

Bernard Well, all these jobs going. Interest rates. Repossessions. Fear of inflation. Foreclosures.

Humphrey Oh yes. Terrible.

Bernard You don't sound terribly worried, Sir Humphrey.

Humphrey Bernard, I am not being sacked, repossessed, inflated or foreclosed. Neither are you.

Bernard Nor's the Prime Minister. But he's worried stiff.

Humphrey So he should be.

Bernard You don't sympathise with him?

Humphrey That's the deal. That's how Prime Ministers' careers go. They get to be on the front page every day for years, which they love. They travel the long path from euphoric triumph to ignominious failure and then make way for the next saviour of the nation. It's called democracy.

Bernard It beats me why anyone would want to be Prime Minister.

Humphrey It's the only top job that requires no previous experience, no training, no qualifications and limited intelligence.

Bernard Sir Humphrey . . . You do believe in democracy, don't you?

Humphrey Do I, Bernard? Actually no, not as most people understand it. Democracy should not be about executing the will of the people. It should be the process whereby we secure the consent of the people to the policies of those qualified to decide on their behalf.

Bernard Like who?

Humphrey Like us, Bernard.

Bernard I believe in democracy, Sir Humphrey.

Humphrey It does you credit. And if all the voters were as informed and intelligent as – say – me, or even you, it could possibly work. But that's hardly realistic.

Bernard Well, obviously we have to stop the government making stupid mistakes. If I did everything the Prime Minister told me to do, I'd be fired within a week, and rightly so. But I *am* there to help him.

Humphrey Bernard, we have a leadership crisis in this country. If the government can't or won't exercise it, it falls to us, whether we want it or not.

Bernard I know. Power abhors a vacuum.

Humphrey And we are currently led by one. We should exercise power because we have nothing to gain or lose personally: we have respectable salaries, honours, an office and a chauffeur . . .

Bernard I haven't got a chauffeur . . .

Humphrey You will, Bernard, when you grow up. We end up with an index-linked pension, a bank directorship, a couple of nicely remunerated quangos and a cottage in the Dordogne. So we can be entirely even-handed in our judgements and make them in the public interest.

Bernard Well, things may not seem so bad soon, when we tell the Prime Minister about Kumranistan.

He taps the file on the coffee table.

European Central Bank to the rescue.

Humphrey Bernard! Do not mention the ECB to the Prime Minister. You know his views.

Bernard I know he's afraid that Brussels will take away most of his powers.

Humphrey They already have. And so they should. All we need him to do is preside at tonight's dinner, pretend he's read the Kumranistan plan, and leave the rest to us.

Jim Hacker, the Prime Minister, enters right. He is followed by a Driver carrying a pile of five Red Boxes.

Jim Sorry I'm late, it's been a terrible day.

Humphrey Any particular reason?

The Driver leaves.

Jim You've read about the Cabinet split?

Humphrey Yes.

Jim You've seen what's happened to the Footsie and the pound?

Humphrey Yes.

Jim So how many particular reasons do you want?

Humphrey Well . . .

Jim And now this Lancaster House conference is turning into a catastrophe.

Humphrey It was your idea to convene it, Prime Minister.

Jim Humphrey, if you become President of Europe in the middle of the biggest financial crisis for a generation –

Bernard Um – with respect, Prime Minister, there is a President of the European Union and it's not you. What the UK Government currently has – not you personally – is the Presidency of the European Council.

Jim He's President of the Union, I'm President of the Council.

Humphrey No, Prime Minister, the President of the European Union itself is the Belgian Prime Minister . . .

Jim Who is completely unknown!

Humphrey Well, obviously! He's Belgian.

Jim And not elected. Appointed. In secret! Course, you wouldn't have a problem with that, would you, Humphrey?

Humphrey You do me an injustice. I am all in favour of elections. Provided the right people do the voting. But the difference, as far as you're concerned, is between being head of an empire of five hundred million people and chairing the Council of Ministers for six months.

Jim Humphrey, we were talking about why I convened the conference on this dreadful recession. I had to do something.

Humphrey And the conference was something. So you did it! Well done.

Jim But now it's falling apart, which might just finish me.

Humphrey It may not be falling apart, Prime Minister.

Jim Haven't you been reading the conference reports?

Humphrey *I* have. Have you?

Jim The spadework wasn't done properly. The Foreign Secretary and the Chancellor let me down badly. Instead of having everything nailed down before they all convened, they left it to chance. Useless! We only just won re-election and they're plotting to get rid of me already!

Bernard '*Forsan miseros meliora sequentur.*'

Jim What?

Bernard 'For those in misery, perhaps better things will follow.'

Humphrey Well said, Bernard.

Bernard I didn't actually say that. That was Virgil.

Humphrey I know that, Bernard.

Bernard At least I did say it, just now, but not originally.

Humphrey Thank you, Bernard. We get the point.

Jim It was completely predictable: the Krauts don't want a stimulus plan, they're terrified of runaway inflation, that's what destroyed the Weimar Republic and brought them Hitler. The Wops and the Dagoes are up to their armpits in debt already. The Frogs only want it if France gets all the benefits . . .

Bernard (*interrupts*) Prime Minister, I really think you should stop using these pejorative epithets to describe our allies, they might slip out in public sometime.

Jim Quire right, Bernard. Thank you. And the Micks and the Polacks aren't getting the subsidies they were promised, which they regard as a betrayal. So it's time for me to get hands-on and give some leadership.

Humphrey Good.

Jim So – tell me, what should I do?

Humphrey That's just the kind of leadership we need.

Jim Thank you. Humphrey.

Humphrey And we have good news for you, Prime Minister . . .

Bernard Late last night we had a breakthrough at Lancaster House. A new player appeared on the scene.

Jim The Americans? Are they coming after all?

Humphrey No, their position is immutable. They won't come to the conference because you wouldn't let them chair it.

Jim I can't let them chair a European conference, Humphrey. Look at the map!

Humphrey It could become an international conference, if that would save the whole European financial system from melting down again.

Jim Don't be silly, Humphrey. I'd lose face.

Humphrey Oh yes, of course. Silly me.

Bernard Prime Minister, Kumranistan has joined us.

Jim Has it? Good. (*A beat.*) Have I heard of them?

Humphrey They have oil. Massive new reserves have been found. They're offering a possible ten-trillion-dollar loan to Europe. Secured against future purchases.

Jim But – that could solve everything.

Humphrey Yes.

Jim Save the conference!

Bernard Yes.

Jim Save Europe, in fact! (*In his own world.*) 'TRIUMPH FOR PRIME MINISTER!' 'VICTORY FOR PRESIDENT OF EUROPE!'

Humphrey With respect . . .

Jim (*firmly*) Victory for a *President of Europe*, Humphrey.

Bernard It might even save your job.

Jim My job's perfectly safe. Other people have survived with small majorities. Wilson had a majority of four in 1964. He lasted six years.

Humphrey I was never awfully good at sums but – um, four would be exactly double the size of your majority, am I right?

Jim So?

Humphrey He had to fight a second election pretty soon, to get a working majority.

Bernard And Wilson had hair.

Jim (*dangerously*) What are you saying, Bernard?

Bernard Nothing. Only that . . . well, no Prime Minister or US President has been elected without a full head of hair since Eisenhower or Churchill in the 1950s. So I'm, um, saying that you did magnificently to win a majority of two.

Jim (*bitterly*) I had hair when I was first elected. I lost my hair in the service of my country.

Humphrey The Kumranistan deal may solve your problems.

Jim Fine. Where do I sign?

Humphrey We're not quite there yet. They want something in exchange.

Bernard You know where Kumranistan is?

Jim Yes. (*A beat.*) Well, sort of. You know, over there.

Bernard It lies in Turkestan, north of Kazakstan, Uzbekistan, and Afghanistan. (*Goes to a globe.*) Here, in fact.

Jim As I said. Exactly.

Humphrey They had been planning to take their oil to Europe through the Soviet pipeline.

Jim They're not Soviets any more, Humphrey. They haven't been Soviets for twenty years.

Humphrey They still are in spirit, and always will be.

Bernard The, um, Russians want a pretty huge payment –

Humphrey Which Kumranistan doesn't want to pay, since the Soviets will have their hands on the pipeline tap.

Bernard So, with a little prompting from us: Plan B! A pipeline through Turkey, Greece and southern Europe, avoiding Russia altogether.

Humphrey What they need is European agreement. And that's what they're prepared to lend us ten trillion dollars for.

Jim Why?

Humphrey They want the guarantee of future oil purchases by everyone in the EU.

Jim (*a beat*) I don't get it.

Humphrey It's awfully simple, Prime Minister. Kumranistan will lend Europe the money to buy Kumranistan's oil.

Jim And Europe borrows another ten trillion? More debt?

Humphrey It's not a problem, it doesn't have to be repaid for years. We get the money now, interest free, and we repay it in the future when we buy the oil that we'll need anyway.

Jim So where do they make their money?

Humphrey We'll pay a premium on the oil. But that's not for many years.

Jim Are all the Europeans on board?

Humphrey They are. And the problems are what we've been negotiating, as you will have seen in your Red Boxes.

Jim Yes. Um – remind me.

Humphrey Well, as you'll doubtless remember, the Turks refused to cooperate unless they were admitted to the European Community. I see their point. I've always had a soft spot for Johnny Turk.

Jim Johnny Turk? (*Sniggers.*) You're on first-name terms, then?

Humphrey (*laughs mirthlessly*) Very droll, Prime Minister. Turkey is an important ally, the only Muslim country with a secular democracy. We *need* –

Jim (*interrupting*) – Johnny Turk, yes.

Bernard Germany, France and Italy were against the plan on principle.

Jim What changed their minds?

Humphrey A ten-trillion-dollar loan.

Bernard That surprised me, Sir Humphrey. Surely, if a principle was involved . . . ?

Humphrey I think you'll find ten trillion dollars is a bit above the going rate for principles in the EU, Bernard.

Jim What *was* the principle?

Humphrey They don't like Muslims.

Jim Oh. Ah.

Bernard Anyway, everything is agreed. Everyone gets a share in the construction.

Bernard unfurls a big wall map. It shows an absurd zig-zag pipeline route through Turkey, Bulgaria, Romania, Greece, Macedonia, Albania, Serbia, Montenegro, Bosnia, Hungary, Slovakia, Czech Republic, Austria, Croatia, Italy, Spain, France, Germany and all points north.

Here's the route. That helped, of course,

Jim We're saved! But why didn't I know about all this?

Humphrey It's top secret.

Jim Good God, Humphrey, I'm the Prime Minister!

Humphrey (*soothing*) I know, Prime Minister, and what an excellent Prime Minister you are! But it had to be kept under wraps. If it had leaked this week, money markets would have gone mad . . .

Jim I see. Well . . . is that everything I need to know?

Bernard There's one other thing.

Humphrey (*warning*) Bernard . . .

Jim gives Humphrey an inquiring look.

Bernard A power group in Kumranistan still wants the Russian route.

Humphrey Ah. (*Relaxes.*) Yes, Bernard's right, they don't want to upset the Soviets. It's understandable, they share a border. But the Kumranistani Foreign Secretary has come over here to put the deal to us if we want it.

Jim Invite him to dinner! Tonight!

Bernard I did, Prime Minister.

Humphrey (*slowly, patiently*) That's why we're here.

Jim And he can do the deal? Now?

Humphrey He has the authority. But he needs careful handling, they're very sensitive about respect.

Jim I know, those Middle-Eastern types . . . (*Chuckles.*) So insecure, always so worried about losing face. (*Catches himself.*) Though sometimes, of course, that's perfectly reasonable. But you get an awful lot of respect for ten trillion dollars. He can have all of mine, for a start.

Humphrey Excellent, Prime Minister.

He exits. Bernard is following.

Jim Bernard.

Bernard Yes, Prime Minister?

Jim There's something you're not happy about. What is it?

Bernard Oh. Um . . . um . . . I'm not sure I can –

Jim Spit it out, Bernard.

Bernard Um – '*Timeo Danos et dona ferentes . . .*'

Jim looks blank.

'I fear the Greeks, especially when they bring gifts.' . . . Remember the Trojan Horse, Prime Minister.

He exits. Jim thinks a moment, gets out his BlackBerry and dials.

Jim Claire? You at Chequers yet? . . . Come to my study please . . . Now!

He rings off, hurries to the pile of Red Boxes, removes the top four and opens the lowest box. He digs out a file from near the bottom. Opens it and starts to read. There is a knock at the other door.

Come in.

Claire enters. She is in her late thirties, attractive and intelligent.

Ah. Claire. There's something I don't know about this pipeline plan. What is it that Humphrey isn't telling me? Bernard was blathering about Trojan Horses.

Claire That's interesting. Must be the pipeline mechanics.

Jim I don't care about the mechanics, I'm not an engineer.

Claire Fiscal mechanics, Jim. Financial engineering. Perhaps Humphrey has arranged for the proposed loan to go through the European Central Bank, and isn't mentioning it.

Jim Is that important?

Claire Yes. What if it's set up so that if we want any of the loan we'll have to join the euro?

Jim We can't join the euro! It would be a catastrophe! Hand over control of interest rates? Control of exchange rates? Control of money supply? When I need to inflate to get re-elected, the ECB might *de*flate because of German price rises and I could get kicked out!

Claire Candidly, I'm not sure if that would bother Sir Humphrey.

Jim And then there's Greece! And Portugal! They could drag down our recovery!

Claire What recovery?

14

Jim (*picks up phone*) Bernard, tell Sir Humphrey that I want to see him . . . No, any time within the next *ten seconds* will do.

He hangs up.

Claire I think I'll disappear.

She slips out stage left. Sir Humphrey knocks and enters.

Jim Ah, Humphrey. About this loan . . .

Humphrey Prime Minister?

Jim It is all good news, isn't it?

Humphrey Tremendous news.

Jim There's no hidden snags? You know. Terms and conditions, penalty clauses, tough guarantees?

Humphrey Oh no. Nothing like that. Standard agreement.

Jim An ordinary Treasury loan? As far as we're concerned?

Humphrey (*hesitates*) In a sense. Yes.

Jim In a sense?

Humphrey In due course. Following agreed procedures. After certain formalities.

Jim But the money goes straight to the Treasury?

Humphrey It goes to the Treasury, yes, of course.

Jim *Straight* to the Treasury?

Humphrey Broadly speaking, yes. More or less.

Jim Broadly speaking? How would you describe it if you were . . . narrowly speaking?

Humphrey is silent.

Does it have to go through the European Central Bank?

Humphrey We get the money, that's what matters.

Jim Let me put this another way. Will the loan be in euros?

Humphrey Prime Minister, I urge you not to clutter your mind with procedural detail and monetary trivia.

Jim Humphrey. In words of one syllable, is this plan dependent on our abandoning sterling and joining the euro?

Humphrey (*chuckles*) 'Dependent' has three syllables and 'abandoning' has four. (*Checks his watch.*) Seriously, Prime Minister, it's almost time for your dinner with the Foreign Minister of Kumranistan, you really mustn't be late.

Jim Answer my question.

Humphrey All right, Prime Minister, you've asked a straight question and I'll give you a straight answer, which, however, clearly has to be considered in its proper context: in the course of all financial negotiations, certain provisos have to be preconditioned, various caveats have to be postulated, designated, investigated and specified and a number of considerations have to be determined, acknowledged and indeed sometimes conceded so that we are able to facilitate the finalisation of preliminary plans to create an epistemological basis for all parties to proceed towards a mutually beneficial consummation which will acknowledge and safeguard the vital interests of all the participants without jeopardising in any material way the underlying collective benefit ultimately accruing to the signatories or leaving unresolved such anomalies and irregularities that might precipitate operational uncertainties down the line, so that there will be a presumed modicum of ironclad reciprocity which in the great scheme of things will be to everybody's advantage.

Jim Did that mean yes or no?

Humphrey Don't you think yes and no are rather broad and unspecific in their application?

Jim No. Is joining the euro a condition of getting the loan?

Humphrey In the sense that . . . if agreement is . . . at the end of the day . . .

Jim *Humphrey!*

Humphrey Yes, it is.

Jim You were going to hide this from me until it was too late!

Humphrey No, but, yes, I mean, they all insisted . . . the ECB insisted . . . Prime Minister, it is the only way! You need this deal. I did it for you.

Jim For me?

Humphrey Prime Minister, I'm trying to save you from yourself.

Jim Humphrey, do you know what comes with joining the euro?

Humphrey The loan, European unity . . .

Jim An austerity package. Disastrous interest rates, public expenditure cuts, more interference from Brussels in every damn thing. No ECB. No euro. Or no deal!

Humphrey All the delegates have so many objections.

Jim Ten trillion dollars' worth of objections?

Humphrey is silent.

As I thought. It would be the ultimate victory for Brussels. Britain becomes a mere outpost of the European empire.

Humphrey Of which you're a President.

17

Jim Don't be silly, Humphrey, I just chair meetings for six months.

Humphrey If you would just take another look at the computer models . . .

Jim No. Computer models got Britain *into* this whole financial mess.

Humphrey That's different. Nobody knew that those computer models in the City were being given faulty information. Everyone assumed the mortgages were worth their face value.

Jim But they were worth nothing! Why didn't anyone know? Why didn't *you* know?

Humphrey (*sighs, humiliated*) Everyone thought that everyone else understood what was going on and nobody wanted to admit they couldn't make sense of it.

Jim Why couldn't they?

Humphrey Because it *didn't* make sense! Everybody thought that all the others knew, and there *were* some who knew, but the ones who didn't know didn't believe that the ones who *did* know knew.

Jim Say that again?

Humphrey Nobody wanted to rock the boat because everyone was making so much money!

Jim Computer models, Humphrey, are no different from fashion models: seductive, unreliable, easily corrupted, and they lead sensible people to make fools of themselves. And because you believed the computer models about the euro you tried to bounce your plan past me, and not tell me until it was too late. I'm appalled. I really don't know if we can go on working together.

Humphrey Prime Minister!

Jim I always thought I could trust you.

Humphrey (*anguished*) You can!

Jim Quite frankly, I'm now profoundly suspicious of this whole pipeline plan. I mean, I don't know what else I don't know. Do you know?

Humphrey Do I know what you don't know?

Jim Yes. Is there anything else I don't know that I should know?

Humphrey Well, I . . . I hardly know where to begin.

Jim About this plan, I mean!

Humphrey regains control of himself.

Humphrey Prime Minister, you know everything that you need to know. If you want the loan, if you don't want your premiership to crash on take-off, this is the way it has to be.

Bernard knocks and enters.

Bernard Drinks with Mr Aitikeev, the Kumranistani Foreign Secretary, are in five minutes, Prime Minister.

Jim Thank you, Bernard. At least I can believe what you tell me.

Jim looks at Humphrey, and exits.

Humphrey Shut the door.

Bernard follows, shutting the door from outside. From inside:

Did you tell the Prime Minister about joining the euro?

Bernard Absolutely not, Sir Humphrey. You told me not to.

Humphrey Well, what put him on to it?

Bernard Perhaps it was his Special Adviser.

Humphrey That woman! How did she get here without our knowing?

Bernard I expect he called her on his BlackBerry.

Humphrey Bernard! You're letting him make his own appointments? If you lose control over his diary, you lose control over him! You never know where it'll end. He'll start running the country.

Bernard He can't. He doesn't know how to.

Humphrey Of course he doesn't. So he must be stopped.

Bernard But what can I do about it?

Humphrey Get rid of his BlackBerry, Bernard!

Bernard How?

Humphrey Look. Give me yours.

Bernard hands over his BlackBerry.

Get me a paper clip.

Bernard gets one from Jim's desk. Humphrey straightens it.

You slide off the back plate. Take out the battery. See that hole? It's the reset button.

Push it in there. Right. Now it's scrambled for days.

Bernard takes back his BlackBerry and checks it. Humphrey is right.

Bernard Sir Humphrey! I had no idea you understood technology.

Humphrey I understand survival. You can practise while I'm at the dinner.

Humphrey exits.

Blackout.

*Jim and Claire are enjoying drinks after dinner. It is now
dark outside.*

Jim Dinner went well, I thought. They liked my speech.

Claire And they *really* liked the goulash and dumplings.

Jim (*gives her a look*) What did you make of the
Kumranistani Foreign Minister? You think he's really
going to come up with this loan?

Claire With the Kumranistanis, it's all about personal
relationships. Trust. Confidence. Respect. Plus, he really
liked the goulash so that's a good start – so much better
than the usual rubber chicken.

Jim Then all we'll need is a few endorsements.

Claire Endorsements?

Jim Yes. Do you remember the World Economic Forum
at Davos? That really worked because Bob Geldof came
out in support of it.

Claire Yes, we're working on that. And Annie Lennox,
and Bono.

Jim Bono. Great!

Bernard enters.

Hello, Bernard. Enjoy dinner?

Bernard I wasn't there, I was busy with – other things.

Jim Pity, you'd have enjoyed my speech.

Bernard I'm sure, Prime Minister, but I heard the goulash
was good.

Jim (*gives him a look*) New cook.

Bernard Yes, and in connection with that, we have a situation. We've just discovered the cook here is in the UK illegally.

Claire (*instantly alert*) We have an illegal immigrant working at Chequers?

Jim How? What the hell is the Home Office doing?

Bernard I wonder if anyone will ever solve that perennial riddle.

Jim Plotting against me, I should imagine. The Home Secretary wants my job too.

Claire They all do.

Jim I'll reshuffle her to the graveyard: the Ministry of Culture, Media and Sports. There's no coming back from there.

Bernard I've never understood the connection between those three.

Jim Culture, Media and Sports? None of them matter.

Claire But if you suck up to them you get lots of good publicity.

Bernard What do I do about this cook?

Jim Where's she from?

Bernard She wouldn't say, apparently, but she's got a false EU passport.

Jim Can't we just rush a visa through for her?

Bernard I'll try, but if you're right about the Home Office it'll take months. I think we have to let her go.

Jim Right. We can't risk the media finding out. 'PRIME MINISTER HARBOURS ILLEGAL IMMIGRANT!' How did it come to light?

Bernard One of the waiters mentioned it at dinner.

Jim Somebody's probably phoned the BBC already.

They all laugh.
The phone rings. Bernard answers it and listens.

Bernard Hello . . . It's the BBC . . . Oh, I see. Fine . . . Ah! (*He hangs up.*) That was actually the Press Office. BBC Television's devoting their Sunday morning programme to you, Prime Minister.

Jim Devoting it to me?

Bernard No other stories. A full hour about you.

Jim Should I be pleased?

Bernard I fear not. It will be called *Government in Crisis*.

Jim Christ!

Bernard They want to interview you about the rumoured Cabinet reshuffle and the deadlock in the Lancaster House Conference.

Claire You're not going to do that, Jim. (*To Bernard.*) He's not doing that.

Jim If I could mention the Kumranistan loan . . .

Claire You can't! Not until Kumranistan has definitely signed on the dotted line and not until this euro business with the European Central bank is sorted out.

Jim Phone them back. Pretend to be helpful.

Claire Whatever they ask, just give them one of the replies in the red binder by the phone.

Bernard crosses to the phone and peruses the red binder with interest.

Bernard I haven't seen this before.

Jim Supplied by the Press Office.

Claire At my suggestion. I worked on it with them.

Bernard Good. (*Dials.*) Yes . . . May I speak to Robin Simpson? (*Listens.*) Yes, it's Bernard Woolley here, the Prime Minister's Principal Private Secretary . . . He can't speak to you himself, but how can I help?

He presses the speakerphone button, so that Jim and Claire can hear.

Robin (*voice-over*) Well, it seems that he is losing the support of his Cabinet and backbenchers.

Claire Number three.

Bernard turns a page and reads a reply from the red binder.

Bernard 'The Prime Minister is not interested in Westminster tittle-tattle. He has the full support of his colleagues and his party on all matters of substance. It's business as usual.'

Robin (*voice-over*) I see. But has the Prime Minister thought of resigning in the interests of party unity?

Claire Number four.

Bernard (*as he turns the page*) You're *seriously* asking me that?

Claire lip-mimes along with him.

'The Prime Minister was elected to do a job and he intends to get on with it. It will mean tough decisions but that's what the country expects and that's what he's going to do.' Next?

Robin (*voice-over*) What about the awful state of the economy?

Jim *and* **Claire** Number one.

Jim now lip-mimes along with Claire.

Bernard 'This isn't a British crisis, it's a world crisis. Many countries are worse affected than we are. We intend to play our part within the community.'

Robin (*voice-over*) But what exactly is he doing about it?

Jim Two?

Claire nods.

(*To Bernard.*) Two.

Bernard 'The government will do everything that needs to be done. He will not flinch from his duty and a statement will be made when the time is ripe.'

Robin (*voice-over*) Why do you think the European Financial Conference has got nowhere?

Bernard I don't think that.

Jim *and* **Claire** Five.

Bernard What?

Jim *and* **Claire** FIVE!

Robin (*voice-over*) Is the Prime Minister there?

Bernard No, sorry, that's the TV you can hear.

He mouths 'Shut up!' as he switches off the speakerphone.

Um . . . (*Flipping page to read number five.*) 'The meeting stroke conference has certainly not been a failure. There has been invaluable groundwork and a blueprint is being drawn up for the next phase. Rome wasn't built in a day.' (*Listens.*) Thank *you*.

Jim What's she thanking you for?

Bernard (*hand over mouthpiece*) She says I've been thoroughly unhelpful.

Jim Well done, Bernard.

Bernard (*into phone*) What? . . . How happy is the Prime Minister about his future?

Jim I'm as happy as a ratcatcher on a rubbish dump.

Bernard The Prime Minister is as happy as an Environmental Health Officer on a Civic Amenity Site.

He hangs up.

Jim I hate the BBC. Always waxing indignant. Nasty, rude, arrogant, aggressive, ungrateful people who all think they could do better than me. They have their own political line. It's like having three Oppositions: one at Westminster and two others at Broadcasting House and the TV Centre.

The phone rings. Bernard gets it.

Bernard Yes? . . . Oh, Ms Simpson again . . . What kind of leak? . . . About joining the euro?

Jim and Claire are all ears.

No, the Prime Minister knows nothing about this. Britain's position on the euro is unchanged . . . No, I can't explain the markets, who can?

He rings off.

Jim Let's get online.

He picks up his BlackBerry from his desk, where he left it before dinner.

My BlackBerry doesn't seem to be working.

Bernard (*pretending surprise*) Good heavens! Mine isn't either.

Claire Mine is. Oh. This is interesting. The rumours started after heavy buying of euros by Golding Brothers Bank. Funny.

Jim Why?

Claire Humphrey's got a directorship lined up there when he retires.

They all look at each other.

Jim He's out of control.

Bernard It might have been someone else.

Jim Who else knew? Even I didn't know.

They all think.

Bernard Shall I get Sir Humphrey?

Claire Has he gone to bed?

Bernard When last seen, he was drowning his sorrows in a glass of The Glenlivet in the Long Gallery.

Jim (*still thinking*) As there's been heavy buying of the euro . . . that would explain today's heavy selling of the pound. I must *do* something. (*He does nothing.*)

Bernard You know, I'm sure Humphrey wouldn't leak.

Jim Are you?

Bernard No.

Jim He tried to bounce us into the euro and feather his nest by briefing the bank. I've got to get him under control. He's an over-mighty subject.

Bernard Actually, he's the Queen's subject, not yours, you're just the –

Jim I know who I am, Bernard! Claire, it's just one more example of the corruption of those who think they're above the law. We've started to curb the MPs, now we must deal with the Civil Service.

Claire Suits me. We've had that paper ready for a while.

Bernard What paper?

Claire Reform of the Civil Service, root and branch.

Bernard Oh! That paper.

Jim So we have. Where is it, Bernard?

Bernard (*immediately*) It's gone.

Jim What do you mean, 'gone'?

Bernard Lost. Discredited. Shredded. One of those. Can't remember exactly.

Jim Bernard . . .

Bernard It really wasn't very good. Too general. Badly argued. Impracticable. Over-specific . . .

Jim Too general *and* over-specific?

Claire There's a copy in your desk, Jim.

She gets it. Jim leafs through it.

Jim Oh yes. (*Chuckles.*) That will really cramp their style. Clip their wings. (*Chuckles.*) Tie their hands.

Bernard Nothing has hands and wings, Prime Minister.

Jim Sorry, Bernard, but the party will love this. So will the MPs. It'll deflect attention from all their little fiddles and diddles. Get Humphrey in, Bernard.

Bernard exits, gloomily.

The country will love it too. It's a winner.

Claire Jim, just remember the old rule: never corner the rat, it may bite. Give him an escape route.

Jim nods. Bernard re-enters.

Bernard He's coming.

Humphrey enters.

Jim Ah, Humphrey, sit down. We've been talking about this leak.

Humphrey What leak, Prime Minister?

Jim About joining the euro. Surely you've heard? It's all round the City, apparently.

Humphrey Oh. That. Yes, well . . .

Jim What can you tell me about it?

Humphrey I, Prime Minister? Nothing, except I'm told there are these rumours. Happens all the time.

Jim This is different. Hardly anybody knew your plan. Then Golding Brothers Bank started buying wads of euros this afternoon. Who tipped them off?

Humphrey If anyone did, we'll never find out.

Jim Oh, I think we will. Um – where did you have lunch yesterday, Humphrey?

Humphrey I can't remember.

Bernard It was Le Gavroche, Sir Humphrey.

Humphrey Oh yes, Le Gavroche. Why?

Jim On your own?

Humphrey I, er, I don't recall . . . Now who *was* it?

Jim You don't remember that either?

Humphrey One has so many lunches.

Jim (*helpfully*) One a day, in fact.

Humphrey Yes.

Jim I understand. Bernard, ring Le Gavroche and ask the Head Waiter who Sir Humphrey had lunch with yesterday.

Bernard gets up, heads for the phone.

Humphrey Oh yes, I remember now. Some friends.

Jim Who were they?

Humphrey Just friends.

Jim Not directors of Goldings Brothers Bank?

Humphrey Prime Minister, one does not cross-examine one's friends about what directorships they may happen to hold.

Jim Well, we can easily find out. Anyway, that's not the point.

Humphrey No, of course it's not . . . What *is* the point, exactly?

Jim The point is, there is bound to be suspicion in cases like this.

Humphrey I can't see why. Surely you know, Prime Minister, that the Civil Service will always do what is best for the country.

Jim What about the government?

Humphrey I presume the government will too.

Jim Right. And this air of suspicion isn't fair on loyal public servants.

Humphrey It certainly isn't.

Jim So I've decided to introduce a new Civil Service Act.

Humphrey What?!

Jim Yes, I think you'll be very happy about this. It will include a ban on any related jobs for civil servants for five years after they retire. No revolving door any more. Gone for good.

Humphrey But . . . Prime Minister . . .

Jim No paid directorships, or quangos, no paid consultancies . . .

Humphrey But that's absurd! Men of great wisdom, great experience, leading figures of their generation, so much to offer . . .

Jim And they can offer it, Humphrey. Pro Bono. Latin, Bernard.

Bernard Pro bono publico, actually.

Jim Exactly. All that wisdom and experience can be offered to the unpaid voluntary sector, Humphrey, for the public good. It will remove all temptation to betray government confidences to commercial employers. That'll be a relief, won't it?

Humphrey But there's never been a problem. We have a clearance committee. Everybody's new job has to be approved by it.

Jim Who appoints the members?

Humphrey Um . . .

Bernard There's an established procedure . . .

Claire You appoint them, Sir Humphrey.

Humphrey Do I? Oh yes, so I do. As it happens.

Jim So that will be another burden off your shoulders. We'll appoint an independent Clearance Czar.

Humphrey Not another czar, please, Prime Minister. In the last three years we've appointed an Enterprise Czar, a Youth-Crime Czar, a Welfare Supremo, a

Pre-School Supremo, an Unemployment Watchdog, a Banking Regulator, a Science and Technology Supremo and a Community Policing Czar. If you go on like this you won't need a Cabinet.

Jim Perfect!

Humphrey Perfect? Prime Minister, we even have a Twitter Czar!

Bernard His appointment was announced as a Tweet.

Humphrey What's *he* supposed to achieve?

Jim The same as the others: at least twelve column inches in every paper. Merely by announcing them, it was achieved – it showed we were responsive, we were doing something, and it shut the press up. *And* – it didn't cost anything.

Humphrey The Twitter Czar earns a hundred and sixty thousand a year!

Jim Cheap at the price. Headline news everywhere.

Bernard It would have cost much more if we'd set them up with offices and staff.

Claire But that would have meant more index-linked pensions, which is something else that the Civil Service Act will address.

Bernard Prime Minister, may I urge you, '*Medio tutissimus ibis.*' Moderation in all things. Ovid, of course.

Jim I'm being moderate.

Humphrey Get rid of index-linked pensions? You wouldn't want to do that to the nurses, would you? Or the dedicated teachers, the courageous policemen, the gallant firemen . . .?

Claire The starving Permanent Secretaries?

Humphrey (*laughs mirthlessly*) Very droll, dear lady. Prime Minister . . . I agree that there are aspects of the organisation and administration of the public sector which could certainly benefit from measured consideration in the context of changing circumstances and the structural metamorphosis precipitated by the communications revolution, but it is important to bear in mind that, *exceptis excipiendis*, administrative practical conditions of service have evolved over many years with manifold and complex interrelationships, and any attempt to vary one of them could have serious and unforeseeable effects on others, so to that end I would propose setting up a series of interdepartmental committees . . .

Jim No, Humphrey! No time for interdepartmental committees. But there is one other change that I'd welcome your views on.

Humphrey Prime Minister?

Jim Would you call yourself a generalist? With your degree in classics?

Humphrey Indeed I would, Prime Minister. First Class degree, actually.

Bernard Me too.

Jim You see, I was over at the Ministry of Defence yesterday. I find them rather impressive, don't you?

Humphrey (*wary*) I do, Prime Minister.

Jim What was really impressive was that they knew what they were talking about. They were qualified professionals. Soldiers, generals, admirals, experienced commanders . . . All our other government departments are staffed by historians and literature graduates – and classicists.

Humphrey Excellent. Men with the wisdom of the ages.

Jim No, Humphrey. Amateurs.

Humphrey Amateurs?!

Jim We should have teachers at the Department of Education, doctors and nurses at the Department of Health, accountants and actuaries at the Treasury. Experts. People who actually know what needs to be done.

Humphrey I think that would be very dangerous, Prime Minister.

Jim We would still need generalists to take a broader view –

Humphrey Indeed.

Jim – and we have them: we politicians are the generalists. We need experts to advise us, not more amateurs like me.

Humphrey With respect, civil servants are not very much like you and we do know how to run things.

Jim I want advice from real people, who live in the real world doing the real jobs –

Humphrey Prime Minister, you're striking at the very heart of our whole system of government. Our success is founded upon staying free from the taint of professionalism. And the corruption of specialist knowledge. You're not seriously – you *can't* be serious – it's out of the question . . . You wouldn't really do this? Would he, Bernard?

Bernard shrugs helplessly.

Jim I would. If we're not getting the Kumranistan loan we won't be needing parliamentary time this session to pass a special Finance Act, so we could pass the Civil Service Act instead.

There's light at the end of the tunnel.

Humphrey Ah. You mean, if the European Central Bank agreed that the loan could go direct to the individual countries . . . ?

Jim In their chosen currency . . . Yes, the Civil Service Act would go on the back burner. But you said they wouldn't agree.

Humphrey I didn't *think* they'd agree . . . But I could be wrong.

Jim (*smiling beatifically*) Say that again?

Humphrey (*tight-lipped*) I said, 'I could be wrong.' (*Stands.*) Leave it with me, Prime Minister. Bernard!

Humphrey stalks out, with Bernard trailing unhappily behind him.

Claire Well played, Jim. Bernard's in trouble, though, for not heading this off.

Jim Do you think Humphrey can square the Central Bank?

Claire Yes. The Europeans don't give a toss how the money arrives as long as there's a lot of it and they get it quickly.

Jim So all that business about joining the euro . . . ?

Claire I think it was just a try-on.

Jim Why is he so keen on Europe?

Claire The whole Civil Service is. It moves power away from the politicians and voters and over to appointed commissioners and unelected officials. Like him.

Jim Is that why he leaked this to his banking chums?

Claire No, I doubt if he meant to. I expect he was just sucking up to them, showing how useful he could be. He was probably horrified when they started buying euros.

Jim He's going to have some explaining to do when they realise we're not joining.

Claire He'll find a way.

A knock on the door. Humphrey enters.

Humphrey I've had a quick word with the head of the ECB, Prime Minister. He's talking to everyone.

Jim Good. So, if they all agree, we may actually have this loan in place. Nothing else can go wrong tonight, can it?

Humphrey I don't see how, Prime Minister.

Bernard hurries in, looking worried.

Bernard Prime Minister –

Jim Cheer up, Bernard, have a drinkie, it looks as though your index-linked pension may be safe after all.

Bernard No, Prime Minister – I'm – um – I'm afraid we have a . . . a situation.

Jim Can't it wait till the morning?

Bernard No, it can't. We have a problem. With the Kumranistan Foreign Secretary.

Claire Mr Aitikeev?

Jim Nice chap.

Bernard Yes – well . . .

Bernard shuts the door.

He just buttonholed me in the hall. It seems that Mr Aitikeev wants us to provide a . . . um, sexual partner for him for tonight.

Jim What a prat.

Claire That's really not our problem, Bernard. Or yours.

Jim I always said he was a prat, didn't I?

Bernard Yes, Prime Minister.

Humphrey Boundaries have to be drawn, Bernard.

Bernard I know. Sir Humphrey – Prime Minister – with respect, it *is* our problem. I . . . I confess I didn't handle it as diplomatically as I should have. I'm afraid he felt slighted. He indicated that unless we find him what he wants he won't sign the contract tomorrow.

Claire What?!

Jim My God!

Humphrey How did this happen?

Jim Why didn't you say you'd try to find him someone?

Bernard I should have but, frankly, I was a little shocked.

Humphrey You always were a prig, Bernard.

Bernard (*judicious agreement*) Yes.

Claire So go back to Mr Aitikeev and tell him you're working on it.

Bernard How, exactly?

Humphrey Yes, how, exactly? This is Chequers, not Soho.

Claire Surely Bernard can get a girl up from London?

Bernard (*aghast*) Me?

Jim Are you serious? What about all the security at the gate?

Claire Don't use the gate. It only takes twenty minutes from the West End to Chequers by helicopter. They check it before departure, but nobody checks it on arrival.

Jim Don't they? Why not? And where do you suggest we get a chopper at this time of night?

Bernard We do have an RAF helicopter standing by this weekend. The one the Queen uses.

Jim Do I understand this correctly? You want us to bring a call girl here, in the *royal helicopter*? For the Kumranistan Foreign Minister? Would you say that's an appropriate use of taxpayers' money?

Humphrey, Bernard and Claire consider.

Claire Well, we do want the deal signed tomorrow, don't we?

Humphrey and Bernard nod.

Got any better ideas?

Humphrey I think we should talk to Mr Aitikeev about this.

Jim Who should?

Humphrey You should.

Jim I'm not doing it.

Humphrey The Foreign Secretary's his opposite number, but you refused to invite him this weekend. Clearly you should have. Claire can't do it, she's a woman. You outrank him, so it has to be you.

Jim I can't possibly do it. This conversation is for a subordinate. Like you, Humphrey.

Humphrey stiffens at the insult.

I have to be able to deny all knowledge of it.

Humphrey Perhaps you're right. So I suggest that, as Mr Aitikeev spoke to Bernard, and as he's the Private Secretary, Bernard should talk to him. I think that would be the diplomatic protocol.

Bernard Um – I can't seem to recall any diplomatic protocol that specifies the Principal Private Secretary does the pimping.

Jim Well – okay, not you yourself, maybe, one of your people.

Bernard I don't have any people here. And Prime Minister, we absolutely can't let anyone else in on this.

Jim Why not?

Bernard I'm – um, afraid there's more. He has specific – tastes.

Jim You mean, like blonde or brunette?

Bernard Not exactly.

Jim What? You mean, a redhead?

Bernard No, sir.

Claire Well *what*? Big boobs, small boobs, big bum – what?

Humphrey/Jim Is he gay?

Bernard If only it were that simple.

Jim Bernard, what sort of woman does he *want*?

Bernard Not a woman. A girl. A schoolgirl.

They are truly shocked.

Jim We can't possibly condone that.

Bernard Of course not, Prime Minister. So, what do you suggest I do?

Claire Wait! I just want to be clear on this. What does he mean, exactly? A prostitute dressed as a schoolgirl? Or a sixteen-year-old girl who is still actually at school?

Bernard No. He specified an underage schoolgirl. About twelve years old, preferably. Otherwise the whole deal's off.

Jim How *dare* you bring such a disgusting proposition to me?!

Bernard I'm sorry, Prime Minister. Should I have just let the deal and the conference collapse?

Humphrey sits, shaking his head sadly.

Jim How did he mention it? Was he embarrassed?

Bernard He said he was making a request in total confidence. I assured him I'm extremely discreet. He said, 'No, I want it to be in *total* confidence.' 'Fine,' I said. 'No problem.' Then he told me. I thought I must have misheard so I asked him to repeat it. He did. I'm afraid he saw the look on my face. He got angry. Made some threats. Told me to see to it or else.

Jim You should have said it just wasn't possible.

Bernard I did. He said they got a man on the moon, we can get a girl from King's Cross.

Claire I suppose that's technically true.

Jim But hardly the point, Claire.

Humphrey Claire, can Mr Aitikeev really wipe out months of diplomacy?

Claire It wouldn't take much – a word here, a word there, a hint of lost confidence. This whole thing's very finely balanced.

Jim Aitikeev wants this deal, right?

Claire Yes, but he lost face with Bernard. Losing face is a big thing, for simple people.

Jim gives Humphrey a look.

Jim Claire, won't Aitikeev lose face if the deal falls apart?

Claire No. You will.

Jim Why not him?

Claire He's still got the Russian route if he wants.

Jim He certainly won't get any more weapons if he screws us over.

Humphrey Maybe Aitikeev doesn't care about the weapons. Maybe it's just the President who wants them.

Claire Internal repression? That's a possibility.

Jim Doesn't Aitikeev have to account to his President if this all goes south?

Claire Theoretically. But Aitikeev's here, the President's over there.

Humphrey There's another possibility. Maybe Aitikeev's bluffing. Maybe it's a test.

Jim A test? Of what?

Humphrey Of our friendship.

Jim We hardly know him.

Humphrey Precisely.

Claire Hmm . . . a test of the friendship between our two countries . . . ?

Jim All I know is, we have to make this deal stick! What happens if it all falls apart now and Kumranistan gets offended?

Claire That wouldn't be good.

Jim It would not! It's a very unstable region. Nuclear proliferation is spreading.

Humphrey Yes. Proliferating, in fact.

Claire Bernard, did the Kumranistan Ambassador return to London after dinner?

Bernard No, he's staying overnight too.

Jim jumps up, energised.

Jim Good idea. Bring him here, right away.

Bernard (*hurrying to the door*) Yes, Prime Minister.

And he's gone. The door slams behind him. Jim looks at Claire and Humphrey.

Jim Okay. Here's my question: why didn't MI6 warn us that Aitikeev was a pervert?

Humphrey Perhaps they don't know.

Jim (*getting up*) That's their job, isn't it? We could have been blackmailing Kumranistan for donkeys' years, instead of having to give them all those weapons systems.

Humphrey Please don't say it that way. We don't approve of blackmail as an instrument of government policy.

Jim Since when?

Humphrey Blackmail is criminal, Prime Minister. We use leverage.

Claire Leverage is legal. It is simply persuasion, reminding people of a few embarrassing things that we might otherwise help them keep secret.

Jim Very nice of us. What's this Ambassador like?

Humphrey Very good chap. We were undergraduates together at Balliol.

Jim He's a friend?

Humphrey We are friendly.

Jim pours himself a quadruple Scotch with a very small splash of soda.

Jim I wonder . . . if the President of Kumranistan knows about Mr Aitikeev's . . . tastes? Can we find out?

Claire Good point! Shall we get him on the phone?

Jim stares at her.

Jim Wake up the President of Kumranistan in the middle of the night and ask if he knows his Foreign Minister likes shagging schoolgirls? I'm not sure *exactly* what would be gained from that.

Claire Just a thought.

Humphrey Not a very good one, dear lady.

Claire Okay, okay, got any better ideas?

Jim What I meant was, might the Ambassador give us that kind of information?

Humphrey Who knows?

Jim wanders over to the windows, sighs, mops his brow.

Jim Still humid.

Claire Clammy. Hope it rains.

The phone rings. They all look at it.

Hello? . . . No, it's Claire Sutton . . . It's the BBC again . . . I see. Thanks. (*She hangs up.*) Piling on the agony. A big new story about global warming has just broken, they're adding that to the Sunday programme too. Global warming computer models have been proved wrong –

Humphrey How shocking!

Claire The new models show that it's even worse than previously thought. Much more severe. And happening faster.

Jim Is that supposed to be my fault too?

Claire Everything is at the moment. They want to know why the government is dragging its feet on CO_2 emission controls.

Jim (*losing it*) Do we have to deal with that tonight? As well as the collapsing conference, the ECB, the BBC, my treacherous Cabinet, my disloyal Party, your leaks, the illegal immigrant, the run on the pound, the Kumranistani paedophiliac . . .? Is there *anything else*, *anything else* we can pile on me tonight? Oh *yes! Global bloody warming*, thank you very much!

Claire It's just that they're going to add it to the catalogue of your failures.

He gives her a look.

Alleged failures, I mean.

Humphrey Meanwhile, may I suggest that you don't worry too much about global warming?

Jim Right. I can't do anything about that tonight, can I?

Humphrey Tell me, how do they know we're all going to drown in fifty years when the weather forecast was so wrong last Friday?

Jim Because all the scientists agree –

Humphrey So they say. So do the computer models. I know. But why should global-warming computer models be any more accurate than financial ones?

Jim Um . . .

Humphrey Wall Street computer models were designed to prove sub-prime mortgage derivatives were low risk. These computer models are designed to show global warming is getting worse.

Jim Come off it, Humphrey.

Humphrey Remember mad cow disease? Computer models for that proved that we'd be dying in our hundreds of thousands by now. The only thing is, virtually nobody died, did they? Same with the salmonella-in-eggs computer models. Same with swine flu.

Jim You're suggesting . . . what, exactly?

Humphrey Global-warming models leave out nearly all the other possible causes except CO_2. And then they say 'Look, CO_2 has caused all this climate change.'

Jim What other causes are there?

Humphrey If the earth were actually getting warmer, one might start by looking at the sun. Solar activity, water vapour, cosmic rays, sunspots, underwater volcanoes –

Jim *If?* The world *is* getting hotter, the science is overwhelming, everyone knows that.

Humphrey There's been no rise in temperature since 1998.

Jim Really? But it *was* rising, wasn't it?

Humphrey From 1975 to 1998, yes, absolutely.

Jim That's what I mean.

Humphrey But it fell from 1940 to 1975. Even though that was a heavily industrialised period, when CO_2 shot up. And overall the temperature isn't rising at all: the hottest year in the twentieth century was 1934.

Jim *I* read that two thousand five hundred top climate scientists contributed to the last IPCC survey and they all agreed that man-made global warming is a proven fact and trapped greenhouse gases are the cause.

Humphrey Nearly fifty of them agreed. The others didn't, actually. But their views were left out of the summaries given to the press.

Claire Haven't you seen that film of the melting icebergs in the Antarctic?

Humphrey Yes. Beautiful, aren't they?

Claire That's caused by CO_2.

Humphrey No, that's caused by warm water masses from the Pacific.

Claire Why are the polar bears becoming extinct?

Humphrey Are they?

Claire The computer models say they are.

Humphrey But the people who actually go and count them have found more than there were thirty years ago.

Jim For heaven's sake, Humphrey! If it's all such nonsense why does everyone believe it?

Humphrey (*amused*) Hard to understand, I agree. But some scientists believe it, lots of others want the billions of pounds you can get for research that seems to show that global warming is caused by greenhouse gases, and most of the scientists who disagree can't get published. Journalists love shock-horror stories, governments want to look virtuous to the voters, lefties want a way to rubbish big oil, and it makes the tree-huggers, whale-savers, anti-capitalists and everyone at the BBC feel holier than thou and warm and fuzzy inside. What's not to like?

Jim Why hasn't anyone else said all this?

Humphrey They have. No one wants to hear it.

Jim So wind farms don't make sense?

Humphrey (*chuckles*) They certainly do, for all the businessmen who are getting enormous government grants for them. But there isn't enough wind to be practical. The total output of all the UK wind turbines put together is one-fifth of one decent-sized coal-fired power station.

Claire You don't believe in global warming?

Humphrey My job is not to believe or disbelieve. My job is to weigh up arguments and produce answers. That's what the Civil Service is for.

Claire To justify inactivity?

Humphrey We can't do something about everything. In fact we can't do much about anything. But I can give the Prime Minister ways of deflecting awkward questions and minimising the apparent urgency.

Claire He can't say any of this to the BBC. They'd shout him down.

Jim No, they'd let me go on as long as I liked. Then the Home Secretary would send round two men in white coats to take me away.

Claire And the BBC would film it.

Jim Claire, phone the BBC back about global warming and give them a version of number six.

Claire goes to the phone, and dials.

Claire Okey-dokey.

Jim I really think you must be misinformed somewhere. Al Gore got the Nobel Peace Prize for his work on global warming.

Humphrey So did Dr Kissinger for his work on the Vietnam War.

Jim has no answer to that.

Claire Hello? . . . Robin Simpson . . . Claire Sutton here, from Chequers. I've talked to people here about the new global-warming forecasts. I can tell you that the government is taking the latest findings extremely seriously and is monitoring the situation as it develops.

Jim (*ignoring Claire*) You think it's all a scam? I can't get my head around this.

Humphrey For some people it's a scam. For most, it's just the greatest outbreak of collective hysteria since the witchcraft trials in the seventeenth century.

Bernard enters.

Bernard The Ambassador of Kumranistan, Prime Minister.

Jim I'm not ready for him. Oh God!

The Ambassador is entering.

Oh good!

The Ambassador is the ideal diplomat. He has a beard, and an excellent English accent. He is urbane, courteous and never loses his cool. He is wearing silk pyjamas and a monogrammed robe.
Jim greets him like a long-lost friend. Claire hangs up.

Ah. Your Excellency!

Ambassador Prime Minister. Please excuse my *déshabillé*, I had just retired for the night when I received your summons.

Jim No problem. We're awfully casual at Chequers.

Ambassador (*turns to Humphrey*) Ah, Bubbles, my dear chap. It's like the old days, isn't it? Late night drinks and all that.

Jim Bubbles?

Bernard *and* **Claire** Bubbles?

Ambassador They don't know your old nickname?

Humphrey (*mortified*) No, they . . . er . . . a silly thing, Prime Minister . . . I used to be partial to champagne, that's all.

Jim And this is Claire, Head of the Policy Unit at Number Ten.

Handshakes. Jim indicates that the Ambassador should sit. They all sit.

I'm glad to hear that you and Bubbles are old friends.

Humphrey scowls.

Ambassador Yes indeed.

Jim So. Bernard's briefed you?

Ambassador He has.

Jim And?

Ambassador And – what?

Jim Exactly. And *what*?!

The Ambassador looks around for guidance.

Ambassador I'm not sure that I know precisely what you're asking me.

Jim Does Mr Aitikeev mean what he says?

Ambassador Prime Minister, the Foreign Minister consults me on matters of Kumranistan's policy pertaining to the United Kingdom. Mr Aitikeev's sexual proclivities are not a matter of public policy.

Jim Did you know about his perverted tastes?

Ambassador I don't consider it my business.

Humphrey Well, unfortunately he's sort of made it our business.

Ambassador My understanding is that he asked the Prime Minister's Private Secretary to keep it confidential, and the Private Secretary agreed. Now there are five of us discussing it. (*To Bernard.*) Would you say you kept your word?

Humphrey Oh come on, Freddie . . .

Jim Freddie?

Humphrey Bernard couldn't keep it confidential, could he, not after Mr Aitikeev made those threats?

Ambassador I really can't comment. I didn't hear the conversation.

Claire Your Excellency, do you think Mr Aitikeev will renege on his commitment to the pipeline contract if we cannot . . . oblige . . . him tonight?

Ambassador He can be stubborn.

The Brits exchange glances.

Humphrey Has this sort of . . . request been made by him before?

Ambassador No. Well, yes. In Bangkok, I believe, but no one took any notice because that's par for the course there really, isn't it?

Jim Is it?

Ambassador *Isn't* it?

Jim Has this happened anywhere else?

Ambassador Well, Bombay, the Philippines – you know, a few third-world places but . . . that's different.

Claire How so?

Ambassador It's understood.

Jim Is it?

Ambassador *Isn't* it?

Claire (*intrigued*) You're saying, child prostitution is the accepted norm in those places?

Ambassador I wouldn't know if it's accepted or the norm exactly, but it's certainly not unusual. Look, I suspect that my personal opinion is the same as yours. But I am here, not as a moralist, but as a servant of our government.

Jim So you feel you have to defend him.

Ambassador He is a member of the government, and my boss.

Jim But there are moral considerations here.

Ambassador Indeed there are. And in all fairness to Mr Aitikeev, I'm quite sure that he did not ask you to obtain a virgin for him. (*Turns to Bernard.*) Am I right?

Bernard is wondering if he's losing his sanity.

Bernard No, funnily enough, he didn't.

Ambassador As I thought. He'd never do that.

Jim Because?

Ambassador Moral considerations. He would not defile her. He would want a girl who has already been defiled.

Jim That's more moral?

Ambassador In our culture, once a female has been defiled she is worthless. Dishonoured. Her family will not take her back. If they do, they will kill her. Few men would marry her. Her only real future is in a brothel. As a moral society we have no tolerance for that sort of thing.

Claire Not among women, anyway.

Jim Are you suggesting that we are a less moral society than Kumranistan?

Ambassador I would say, we are even *more* rigorous about purity than Great Britain, yes. But in this instance Mr Aitikeev is offering an excellent opportunity to such a girl: he's not ungenerous and I'm sure he will give her hundreds of pounds. That's better than death, wouldn't you say?

Claire Yes, but that's not the choice here. In our culture –

Ambassador Forgive me, but I'm describing our culture. Mr Aitikeev's culture.

Jim But it's wrong.

Ambassador You say tomayto and I say tomahto.

Jim What?

Ambassador You believe your values are right. So do we. You believe you should impose your values on us. Many of my people would like to impose their values on you. I say, live and let live.

Claire Are you a Muslim?

Ambassador I'm a diplomat.

Claire Yes, I know, but apart from that what are you?

Ambassador I am a Libra. And a member of the MCC, of course.

Jim/Humphrey (*doubtfully/encouragingly*) Well, that's good . . .

Claire You don't want to discuss religion.

Ambassador (*smiles*) Dear me, no. I was brought up to believe it was bad manners to discuss religion in polite company, weren't you? It always leads to *so* much trouble. In my country we have several religions, but they live together in harmony.

Humphrey A secular democracy. A bit like Johnny Turk.

Ambassador Exactly, Bubbles.

Jim Claire was just asking because you seem awfully . . . English.

Ambassador Harrow and Oxford, old chap. I know how to play a straight bat.

Humphrey Opening bat for Oxford. Got a blue.

Ambassador The point is, Prime Minister, my government has expressed a willingness to help you obtain a loan that you need.

Jim It's to your advantage too – your government would prefer not to have Russia's finger on the pipeline's jugular, I'm sure.

Ambassador Look, Prime Minister, I shouldn't really be saying this but, frankly, our President is not as pro-Western as Mr Aitikeev and he responds to pressure from our extremists. We have thousands of them in Kumranistan.

Claire How do you define an extremist?

Ambassador Anyone who opposes the government, really.

Jim Fair enough. We've got millions of extremists here, actually.

Ambassador May I be frank?

Jim Even more frank?

Ambassador Oh, I apologise, I didn't wish to sound impertinent or disrespectful. I am merely the messenger, a humble emissary who speaks for the President of Kumranistan, a man who, I must warn you, is not convinced by your desire to force what you call democracy down the throats of the peoples of our region when he can see the dismal results of it here.

Jim You have the nerve to suggest to me that British democracy produces . . . dismal results?

Humphrey He didn't mean that. You didn't mean that, did you, Freddie?

Ambassador No, no, Prime Minister, I was not referring to you, perish the thought! I mean all those who oppose you, who try to intervene in your noble, tireless work for the British people.

Jim He's right, actually.

Humphrey Indeed he is.

Ambassador If I may make a suggestion – ?

Jim nods.

Mr Aitikeev has kindly offered to help you navigate a way out of your many crises. A way that solves your problems, gives you the upper hand in Europe and which saves face all round. All he asks of you is that you indulge one of his little foibles. Show him a little hospitality. A little generosity of spirit. If you were his guest he would do it for you, without a second thought. You wouldn't have even had to ask.

The Brits look at each other, despairing.

54

Let me try to put it in terms that might help: what we need here is a modicum of multiculturalism, a more broad-minded view of cultural differences. Why must you be so judgemental? Be tolerant of human frailty. You have no personal interest here, one way or the other. What does it matter to you?

Claire Let me try and explain, Your Excellency: what you are suggesting is *against the law* in this country.

Ambassador Of course I know that. But governments break laws whenever they perceive that it's in their national interest. Why do you have the SAS and MI6? What are covert operations, in reality, if not lawbreaking operations?

Humphrey We need them. We live in a dangerous world.

Ambassador I know. I'm not being critical. At your level, breaking the odd law is hardly here or there.

Jim Obviously. But there's a child involved here.

Ambassador A teenager, surely. And you are responding as if Mr Aitikeev were asking for *your* daughter, Prime Minister, but he's not. He just wants some waif who could doubtless do with the money. It's up to you, of course, but don't blame me, that's all.

Jim (*fascinated*) Don't you care about the girl?

Ambassador If she were my daughter, I'd care. But my children are safe in Switzerland. I'm sure that yours are in no danger either.

Claire You don't see there's a principle here?

Ambassador No, I'm sorry, I can't seem to see it. Many cultures allow sex at puberty, so long as it is within marriage. In Sweden the age of consent is fifteen.

Others (*derisive*) Well, Sweden . . .

Ambassador In Italy it's fourteen.

Claire / Bernard / Jim That's different! / Hot-blooded! /
It's the Mafia!

Ambassador It's fourteen in Canada too. In Spain it's
thirteen.

Jim / Claire / Bernard Is it really? / Never knew that. /
Awfully young.

Ambassador And in the Vatican it's twelve. And twelve-
year-olds can be married in my country. Not every
country is like Britain, you know.

Jim More's the pity! We believe in protecting our children!

Humphrey (*warning*) Prime Minister . . .

Ambassador *Your* children, certainly. But remember this:
for some years now, Britain has been fighting a war in
a country bordering on mine. How many children have
been killed and maimed there?

*Jim looks at Bernard, Claire and Humphrey, hoping
one of them knows the answer. They don't.*

You don't know? Nor do I. How many more children
will die? Who knows? But I can tell you who cares: their
parents, their families, a few friends perhaps. Nobody
else? Not you . . .

Jim (*outraged*) I *do* . . .

Ambassador No no, Prime Minister, please don't pretend.
It's impossible to care. We can't take it all on board, it's
too much tragedy. Victims become statistics. Not even
that, actually, because nobody's counting them. You, in
the interests of a greater good, as you perceive it, have
authorised action that led to these deaths. And you may
be right. We are your allies in this, the fanatics threaten
us too.

56

Jim So . . . I don't get it. Your problem is . . . ?

Ambassador Your double standards, Prime Minister.
I urge you to be practical. In the great scheme of things,
what does one little teenage girl matter if you can help so
many others and save them from catastrophe?

Jim It would be the first step on a very slippery slope.

Ambassador Down which you have been sliding ever
since you took the job. It's the price of power. This girl's
life, whoever she is, is probably tragic already. But at
least she'll get paid. And as a result unemployment will
drop, oil prices will drop, foreclosures and repossessions
will stop and Europe will be saved from disaster.

He walks to the door, turns.

I bid you goodnight.

He leaves. Bernard shuts the door.

Bernard He's trying to claim some sort of moral
equivalence between his barbaric culture and ours.

Claire There isn't any.

Jim Certainly not.

Bernard Absolutely not.

Jim (*thinks*) Is there, Humphrey?

Humphrey gives a non-committal shrug.

I can't possibly agree to this. Can I?

Bernard Of course not.

Claire Unthinkable.

Jim Can I, Humphrey?

Humphrey gives another little shrug.

But we have to get this deal, or I'm history.

Humphrey How true.

A pause.

Bernard So – um – how do you want me to handle Mr Aitikeev's request?

Claire Look! Let's discuss this question for what it actually is: is it better for one teenager to get fucked than the whole European economy?

Jim If you put it like that, there's no choice.

Claire Quite.

Humphrey Quite.

Blackout.

Interval.

Act Two

SCENE ONE

Jim, Humphrey, Claire and Bernard are where they were at the end of Act One. The action is continuous.

Jim Here's the problem: If we get a girl for him, and it got out somehow, the public would not understand.

Claire You *think*?

Jim Is there a way to neutralise that?

Humphrey Prime Minister, you have always taken a very high moral tone. You're on the record against teenage sex. If you were now to endorse prostitution as an instrument of policy, there's a chance you could be accused of inconsistency.

Jim There are exceptions to every rule. In this case, I'd make a special exception to allow the girl to have *patriotic* sex with Aitikeev. She'd be doing this for her country, for Britain! It would actually be an act of the greatest nobility.

Claire In which position?

Jim Shut up, Claire! Every day we ask our boys and girls in the front line to risk their lives for their country. A tremendous sacrifice. Some of them make the ultimate sacrifice. This is a different front line, a small sacrifice by comparison, yet one so *huge* in its result that it could tip the balance towards peace and security.

Bernard But statutory rape is a crime.

Jim Mr Aitikeev has diplomatic immunity.

Bernard *You* haven't!

Jim I could be prosecuted?

Bernard Conspiracy. Pandering.

Jim Only if I knew about it.

Humphrey But you *do* know about it.

Claire If any of this leaks, he doesn't know. Okay?

Jim Do you think people will believe that?

Claire Why not?

Humphrey There are so many things you don't know, what's one more?

Jim gives him look.

Claire We must frame it differently. You called this statutory rape, Bernard. We avoid that kind of inflammatory language, even in a classified document. Clinton did it with an adult and he got into trouble just for a blow-job.

Humphrey stands.

Humphrey I don't think I wish to be here for this conversation. It is unseemly. (*Goes to the door, turns.*) Prime Minister, take no part in this. Deniability works better if there's a little truth in it.

Jim But speaking hypothetically, what is your view?

Humphrey Obviously, in difficult times, sacrifices do have to be made. Especially by ordinary people.

He exits.

Claire He's right.

Jim Claire, I hear everything you're saying. But – I still have a sort of uncomfortable feeling about this. I know that may sound weird –

Claire No, it's very sweet of you. Very caring.

Jim Thank you.

Claire Sometimes it's hard for a common-sense solution to prevail over ingrained emotional responses, however irrational.

Bernard If we can't call it statutory rape or a blow-job, how should it be referred to?

Jim We must make it sound positive. Like the Yanks did with torture – they called it enhanced interrogation techniques.

Claire How about 'enhanced entertainment techniques'?

Jim It would have worked, but it's been done.

They think.

Bernard Horizontal diplomacy?

Jim Smoking gun.

Bernard Anglo-Kumranistan Liaison Project?

Jim Isn't that a bit of a mouthful?

Claire That's it! A euro-job!

Jim Brilliant. A euro-job!

Claire We may need some way to refer to the girl, too. What do we call someone who gives a euro-job?

Bernard A eurologist?

Jim What if it *does* get out, how will we defend it?

Bernard No! It's impossible. It's reckless. We're not in London. Mr Aitikeev is staying in this house, not at some hotel. If such a scandal were to get out, we couldn't blame the concierge or the porter for finding the girl for him.

Jim There must be somebody to blame. There always is.

Bernard Who? Security is intense. The gates are guarded by the army. Prostitutes in King's Cross can hardly flag down the royal helicopter. Somebody would have had to authorise it.

Jim Yes, you.

Bernard No, Prime Minister, not me.

Jim You'd refuse to obey me?

Bernard No. You give me a signed instruction and I'll execute it.

Deadlock.
A knock at the door. Humphrey enters.

Humphrey The Director General of the BBC is here to see you.

Jim Why?

Humphrey He says he asked for this meeting last week.

Jim looks at Bernard.

Bernard That's right, Prime Minister. You invited him to pop in for a late drink. He's a neighbour.

Jim And neither of you thought of cancelling it when this whole Kumranistan thing came up?

Bernard We couldn't have foreseen Mr Aitikeev's unusual request.

Jim But we haven't finished with . . . (*Racked with indecision.*) What does he want?

Humphrey More money, I suppose, that's what they always want.

Jim (*a new idea*) I suppose we could manage it, if we brought in the Civil Service Act straight away.

Humphrey (*instantly on guard*) I do think it would be unwise to take a precipitate approach to the Civil Service Act, Prime Minister, or the BBC, which is a magnificent organisation, the Rolls-Royce of broadcasting. It all needs mature deliberation, extensive consultation . . .

Jim On the other hand, if we could really cut the licence fee, then the Civil Service Act wouldn't be so urgent. What do you think? I know that you love the BBC . . .

Humphrey It would seriously . . . um –

Jim – show everyone that we're serious about putting money back into the voters' pockets.

Humphrey is silent.

Good, I'm glad to have your loyal support. Show him in.

Humphrey opens the door.

Humphrey Jeremy. Come in.

Jeremy Burnham, the Director General, enters.

The Director General, Prime Minister.

Jim Jeremy. Do sit down. Drinkie? I'm on Scotch.

Burnham Fine. Thanks.

Jim How can I help you? I'm afraid we're a bit rushed.

Bernard gets the two drinks. Claire gets one for herself. Bernard and Claire sit unobtrusively elsewhere. Bernard takes notes.

But I'm glad you're here. I'd like to take the opportunity to talk about this TV programme.

Burnham What programme?

Jim The programme you're running on Sunday, rubbishing me.

Burnham Are we?

Jim Please, let's not play games.

Burnham Look – It's, um . . . not about you specifically, it's – er, it's part of a broad, measured look at the state of the nation.

Jim Rubbishing me, in fact.

Burnham No, no. Fair. Balanced. Responsible.

Jim Humphrey?

Humphrey Perhaps, Jeremy, you don't realise the full extent of this financial crisis?

Jim Anything that destabilises Britain at this juncture would be grossly irresponsible.

Burnham Obviously we don't want to destabilise Britain, as you put it, but we're not the government information service either. We have a duty to reflect all shades of opinion. We are journalists. It's our job to keep the public fully informed. You refused an invitation to appear on it, I understand. That would have ensured that your opinion was represented.

Jim This may come as a big surprise to you, Jeremy, but I don't want to be pre-recorded, edited, quoted out of context and made to look an utter wally.

Humphrey Why don't you postpone this programme at least until the outcome of this Lancaster House Conference is clear?

Burnham I hope you're not putting political pressure on the BBC?

Jim Political pressure? Good heavens, no!

Humphrey Most improper. I'm not even political, just a humble civil servant.

Jim And we truly value the independence of the BBC.

Burnham I'm glad to hear it. But I'm afraid we can't possibly postpone at such short notice, and I can't interfere with content, I'm only the Director General.

Jim (*as if a great light has dawned*) Oh. I see.

Burnham The producers would smell a rat. And they'd leak it.

Bernard Um – just to clarify – a rat can leak, but you can't leak a rat.

Burnham (*irritably*) What?

Humphrey Thank you, Bernard. Most helpful.

Jim So the BBC's smug and self-satisfied pundits are going ahead with their biased and scurrilous attack on the democratically elected government. Got that, Bernard?

Bernard (*writing*) '. . . democratically elected government.'

Burnham (*calm*) No, I'm saying that our team of professional journalists are going ahead with their fair and balanced review of the current political situation. Got *that*, Bernard?

   Bernard nods, still writing.

Jim Let me stop you right there. Humphrey has just come up with a really interesting idea. Haven't you, Humphrey?

Humphrey I, er, I . . .

Jim He says that in these straitened times, making even more cuts in expenditure will be necessary.

Burnham Impossible. We've already cut to the bone. There's just no more we can do.

Jim Humphrey says that we could sell your digital channels, your websites, BBC 2, 3 and 4, all the radio stations except Radio 4, BBC Publications, BBC Worldwide, the BBC Symphony and the other three orchestras and we could cut the licence fee by eighty per cent. That would be such a relief for you.

Burnham But Humphrey, you've always said . . .

Humphrey I know! I *am* a great supporter of the BBC, it's just that –

Jim But you were saying they were overstretched. Weren't you?

Humphrey Well, I . . . well of course, in normal circumstances, it would, naturally, be an entirely different ball game, but yes, if the nation's under extreme fiscal and monetary pressure it could be necessary *inter alia* to consider measures which under different economic conditions would not have been desirable but –

Jim I couldn't have put it better myself. Humphrey pointed out that only about thirty-five to forty-five hours a week on BBC TV is original and distinctive programming. You could get that all on to one channel, easily. That's what Humphrey is proposing, plus one speech radio channel, Radio 4. Aren't you, Humphrey?

Humphrey Well, perhaps the specifics are not so, not so, not so . . .

Jim So, that's pretty well it. You'd be able to keep all your quality programmes and the World Service and all your financial worries would be solved.

Burnham It's a monstrous idea! The BBC is the beacon of world broadcasting. The great bulwark of civilised values against the tide of commercialism.

Jim A beacon of repeats, Hollywood movies, bought-in programmes and bought-in sporting events. Most of what you show on the BBC is no different from what people get on subscription channels, commercial channels, PayTV or sponsorship. That's what you were saying, right, Humphrey?

Burnham You really can't compare a great public broadcasting service with tacky commercial output.

Jim You can compare the programmes. Cookery programmes, make-overs, quizzes, game shows . . .

Burnham Cultural vandalism!

Jim Why?

Burnham Radio 3 . . . classical music . . . ?

Jim Readily available everywhere. You'd be free at last to focus on quality and forget about *Survivor*, *The Weakest Link* and all that optical chewing gum that so obviously doesn't need to be paid for by the taxpayer.

Burnham But Humphrey –

Humphrey Well, you see, Jeremy . . . I mean, I yield to no one in my admiration for your, er, you know . . . I mean, what you say is certainly, at the end of the day, other things being equal, *mutatis mutandis* . . .

Jim And then there's the question of your salary.

Burnham My salary?

Jim What do you earn now? Eight hundred and thirty-four thousand, plus a gigantic expense account. Running a small organisation like the new BBC obviously couldn't command more than about thirty per cent of your current earnings . . . but as you've said, it's not about the money, it's about quality and service.

Burnham Thirty per cent?

Jim You'd still be earning a lot more than me! And Humphrey. Nothing to complain about there.

Burnham The Cabinet would never back you on this.

Jim Actually, that's one thing they'd definitely back me on. When we go on the BBC your presenters just jeer and sneer. At all of us. Posturing opportunists who've never had to take responsibility for anything, following their party line.

Burnham The BBC reports facts and reflects opinions but it does not have any editorial policy.

Jim Maybe, maybe not. But it has a pretty consistent view on a whole lot of issues: immigration, multiculturalism, global warming, joining the euro . . . Anyway, we'll study your comments on this but I think the basic idea is pretty sound. So – (*Stands up.*) I'll wait to hear from you.

Burnham You certainly will.

Jim Incidentally, to change the subject, if I were to give a *live* interview in that programme on Sunday, from Chequers . . .

Humphrey Live? Are you quite sure, Prime Minister?

Jim Yes. So they can't edit what I say. I would feel that the BBC was at least trying to be fair. Especially if the interview was the last item, so that I could answer all the points . . .

Burnham I don't see why we can't manage that. I'll have a word.

Jim Rather a scoop, really.

Burnham Yes. It might be.

Jim It *would* be! Thank you for your time.

Burnham Thank you, Prime Minister.

Bernard shows Burnham out.

Jim He won't cancel the programme, but they'll give me the live interview at the end of it.

Humphrey Live? I admire your courage, Prime Minister.

Jim Oh God! Have I been courageous?

They all nod.

Okay, Humphrey, help me! What will I say?

Humphrey 'Goodbye'?

Claire At least he's bought us some time.

Bernard Time for what?

Jim Time to think of something to say to the BBC. Time to try and keep Mr Aitikeev in this deal!

Claire (*looks at watch*) Talking of which, Jim, it's getting pretty late. If we're going to find a girl for Aitikeev we have to get on with it.

Jim Is there *no* other way?

Claire We could just say no to him.

Jim Can't risk that. Collapse of conference, collapse of backbench support, collapse of Cabinet. Collapse of my career. The biggest disaster since Dunkirk.

Humphrey I think not, Prime Minister.

Jim Name a bigger one.

Humphrey The Freedom of Information Act.

Jim Humphrey, I'm begging you, what's your advice?

Humphrey Well, Prime Minister . . . one hesitates to say this but there are times when circumstances conspire to create an inauspicious concatenation of events that necessitate a metamorphosis, as it were, of the situation such that what happened in the first instance to be of primary import fraught with hazard and menace can be relegated to a secondary or indeed tertiary position while a new and hitherto unforeseen or unappreciated element can and indeed should be introduced to support and supersede those prior concerns not by confronting them but by subordinating them to the over-arching imperatives and increased urgency of the previously unrealised predicament which may in fact now, *ceteris paribus*, only be susceptible to radical and remedial action such that you might feel forced to consider the currently intractable position in which you find yourself.

Jim is nonplussed.

Jim What does he mean, Bernard?

Bernard I, um – I, er, think that he's perhaps suggesting the possibility that you, um, consider your position. Resign, in fact, Prime Minister.

Jim I'm not resigning, Humphrey. And you can consider the Civil Service Act a done deal. So there!

A tense silence. Jim sits heavily on a chair or sofa, sighs and puts his head in his hands.

What would the Americans do about it?

Bernard Shall we ask them?

Jim Not the White House.

Claire How about the CIA? I know somebody at the sharp end.

Claire goes to the phone and dials.

Yes, hi, it's Claire Sutton . . . I'm at Chequers, actually. Fine, but we have a problem and I wondered if you had a view, or any suggestions . . . Here's the thing: the conference here has been going fine till now. Everyone's ready to agree – yes, incredible! I know. But now, unfortunately, Mr Aitikeev . . . yes, the little Kumranistan Foreign Minister arsehole, he's demanding that we get him an underage schoolgirl tonight to have sex with . . . Yes, tricky, any thoughts? . . . We don't have people who do that.

Jim Do what?

She mimes shooting a gun. Jim, Humphrey and Bernard look at her in horror.

Ring off!

Humphrey I'm leaving again!

Humphrey hurries out, with his hands over his ears. Jim calls out.

Jim Good. And don't come back unless you have something constructive to suggest!

The door closes loudly behind Humphrey.

Claire (*cool, on the phone*) No, that won't fly here . . . You think *that* might help?

Jim Get off that line, it's not scrambled!

Claire Any other thoughts? . . . I don't know, it's after ten p.m. here and we don't keep a vicar on the premises.

Jim NOW!

Claire Sorry, got to rush, the PM is calling me. Call you later.

She hangs up. Jim is horrified.

Jim Assassination? Is that what he suggested?

Claire I agree, it's not practical.

Jim It's impractical *and immoral*! We can't just go around murdering the leaders of democratically elected foreign governments.

Bernard We have actually facilitated the Americans in this sort of operation, I believe.

Jim We've never done it ourselves!

Claire Maybe . . . You know, maybe we *should* consider it, if it's what the people want.

Bernard Which people?

Jim Our people, Bernard. Democracy, in case you hadn't noticed, is about giving the British people what they want.

Bernard How would we know what our people want? They haven't been asked.

Claire It's pretty obvious they don't want us to be held to ransom by little perverts like Aitikeev.

Bernard But he was elected. You're saying our democracy trumps theirs?

Jim Obviously. We're responsible to our people, not theirs. But we can't assassinate him – it's unthinkable, it's wrong . . . it's corrupt . . . How would we do it, actually?

Claire It's not practical, we don't have the people to do that sort of thing.

Jim Are you sure?

Claire No . . . but I'm sure we don't have them here, tonight.

Bernard Um – what was that you said about a vicar?

Claire He suggested getting some religious input.

Jim Why do the Yanks bring God into everything?

Claire He's on their side, isn't He?

Jim So what did he suggest?

Claire Pray.

She sniggers.

Bernard Murder, and prayer?

Claire That's the way they do things.

Bernard Aren't Americans odd?

Jim Maybe it's not such a bad idea.

Claire What?

Jim Prayer.

Claire Are you kidding me?

Jim Why not? Nixon used to pray.

Claire Look what happened to him.

Jim kneels. He points to floor.

Jim Bernard!

Bernard kneels, uncertainly. Jim and he close their eyes, clasp their hands in prayer. Claire watches them, pityingly. After a moment, Jim opens his eyes.

Wait. I need to think for a moment. I've never had to ask God's advice about whether or not to supply a teenage prostitute before! He might be offended.

Bernard Not with you, surely. Aitikeev is the sinner here.

Jim That's right. If God gives me the okay, then it can't be a sin. And if He says no, I won't do it. So I'm in the clear, either way.

Bernard But . . . I wouldn't use profane language to God, if I were you.

Jim stares at him.

You know, like the eff word – (*Whispers.*) Don't actually say that Aitikeev wants to eff a schoolgirl.

Jim (*icy*) Thank you for those helpful comments, Bernard.

Bernard I'm just saying that wouldn't be the norm, that's all.

Claire Bernard, I imagine God knows all the four-letter words, in every language. He's supposed to be omniscient.

Jim Right. In which case – (*A realisation.*) He would know about all this already. In fact, He could be waiting to hear from me.

Claire Then I shouldn't keep Him waiting too long, if I were you. He's probably got a lot of other stuff to deal with.

Jim (*on his dignity*) Okay, but I am Prime Minister of the United Kingdom of Great Britain and Northern Ireland *and* a President of the European Union. I think He knows He has to find time for me when I need it.

Bernard I'm sure He does, Prime Minister.

Claire We'll see, won't we?

Jim Come on, Claire! You too.

> *He taps the floor beside him. Reluctantly, Claire kneels. Jim closes his eyes. So does Bernard. She doesn't.*

O God, our rock in ages past, we're all down here at Chequers – as you know already, of course, being omniscient – ready to sign a pipeline contract that could save the EU from imploding. And now, out of the clear blue sky, Mr Aitikeev has demanded et cetera et cetera you know it all, so if we don't get him a teenage prostitute – excuse my language, Lord, but I don't know any other way to put it – he'll renege, the conference will collapse and the opportunity for agreement and harmony and peace on earth – well, in Europe anyway – will be lost. So my question is: which is the greater evil, O Lord? Is it really okay for me to authorise procuring some little scrubber for him to have sex with? I'm having trouble squaring that away. And oh, and by the way, if you do tell me to get him a girl, what do we do with her afterwards? Give her a gong? Or hand her over to the CIA to send to one of those prisons in Poland that don't exist any more? I look forward to hearing from you at your earliest convenience. Amen.

Bernard Amen.

They get off their knees. The other two look at the PM.

Jim How was that?

Bernard Clear, respectful.

Claire Now what?

Jim See if He answers.

There is a huge flash of lightning outside the windows, followed by a loud crack of thunder and sudden rain.

Bernard (*in awe*) Maybe that's it!

Claire Don't be silly, a thunderstorm's been forecast since yesterday.

Jim If it is God, He sounds angry.

Bernard Obviously! Molesting a girl? No way He'll approve.

Claire (*smiles*) People have been turned into pillars of salt for less.

Jim Claire, this is a serious problem!

Claire I agree! So let's find a serious way of tackling it!

Jim We're trying prayer, since we have no other ideas. Okay?

Claire Okay. Is God telling you to get a girl for Mr Aitikeev, or not?

Jim looks out of the window, waits for an answer. There is no more lightning, but some more distant thunder.

Jim I think what He's saying is: search your heart and find a way to do what's right.

Claire What the hell else would you expect God to say?

They look out of the window. They wait. The sky has nothing more to impart.

Jim You know what? I see a way out of this hideous dilemma. (*Suddenly he's a believer.*) Thank you, God!

Claire Are you all right?

Jim I've had an inspiration! I've been trying to think how I could justify doing this for Aitikeev – even if she is a prostitute or a junkie, I couldn't find a way. It's just plain wrong, no matter which way you look at it.

Bernard So . . . ?

Jim Why must it be a British girl?

Bernard What?

Jim Every time I have a meeting with the Women and Equality Unit or Justice for Women, they tell me there's a huge problem in our major cities with sex trafficking. Reports from the Serious and Organised Crime Agency: Russian girls kidnapped, brought to London by the lorry load, beaten up, threatened their families will be murdered if they don't cooperate. Some of them are swindled into coming to the UK for a job, lent money for travel, put in massage brothels and kept there until they repay the money – if ever! So . . . ?

Claire (*soft, delighted*) I see! Get one of them!

Jim No family here. No one'll miss her! Probably doesn't even speak English. Yeah, that's it! We get one that can't speak English. Then there's no way she can tell anyone anything. We give her to Aitikeev tonight, deport her tomorrow. It's done.

Claire No one would ever know. That's perfect!

Bernard How is that perfect? What about human rights?

Jim We can't protect *everybody*, Bernard. We protect our citizens. What's the matter with you?

Claire Collateral damage.

Bernard Weren't you asking God for moral guidance?

Claire I share Bernard's doubts about that. I wouldn't give God the credit. It's your idea, Jim, and it's brilliant.

Bernard We'd be sex-slave traffickers ourselves.

Jim (*irritable*) Look, Bernard, if some underage illegal immigrant has sex with Aitikeev, I'm sorry about it, but if she's not British, she's not my problem.

Claire Bernard, you really are being a little sentimental.

Bernard stares at them, puzzled.

Jim None of this whole thing is my fault. You want to blame somebody, go talk to Aitikeev. But no, you won't do that. So come up with a better plan or shut up and get it done!

Bernard *I* do not believe that women are worthless.

Jim What?

Claire When did Jim say that?

Jim I don't think women are worthless. It was foreigners I was talking about.

Bernard It seemed to me to be the implication of the whole discussion, of everything the Ambassador said. And I personally am most reluctant to break the law and procure a girl for what seems to me an immoral purpose.

Jim Immoral? The future of Europe is at stake, the money supply, mass unemployment . . . ?

Bernard I just think it's not right. This is a moral dilemma that I really don't know how to address.

He sits in another part of the room.

Jim Bernard, ever since this started you've been bleating on about whether or not something's 'right'! We're politicians, not bishops. We don't have the luxury of doing what's right, we're here to serve the public.

Claire crosses, kneels beside Bernard.

Claire It's not easy, I understand that.

Bernard What if we *do* get this deal signed? What if the Prime Minister loses the next election and the next government has a different policy?

Claire There are no guarantees.

Bernard And for no guarantees I'm to be an accomplice in a euro-job?

Jim The deal *will* stick. It will be a treaty. Great Britain will be a signatory and we always keep our word.

Claire We don't, actually.

Jim Well, we often do. And we definitely would in this case.

Claire (*crosses to phone*) Fine. Bernard, *I'll* organise it. Before it gets any later. Who do I phone?

Bernard To get the helicopter?

Claire To get an underage Russian prostitute.

Bernard You don't know?

Claire No. How would I know?

Bernard So how do you think I know?

Jim Let me get this straight. We've finally decided to do this *and you don't even know how?*

Claire Do *you* know how?

Jim (*losing it*) I can't believe this! The TV news shows tell me we're crawling with illegal Russian hookers, and nobody even knows how to *find* one? What is going *on* here?

Bernard (*to Claire*) Try the Vice Squad. They'll know.

Jim (*yelling*) You want to call the Vice Squad and ask them to find a prostitute and put her on the royal helicopter? Have you lost your *mind*? Front-page banner headlines.

Silence. A dog barks outside. Claire crosses to a window. She looks out at something. She looks back at Jim.

Claire I'm just popping out. Back in a minute.

She goes out. We see her go past the window.

Jim What's that about?

Bernard Don't know. (*He peers out of the window.*) She seems to be talking to somebody out there.

Jim Who?

Bernard Can't really see. Trees are in the way.

Jim turns away, shaking his head, despairing.

Jim So. We're stuck.

Bernard turns back from the window.

Bernard Aren't you worried that this is wrong, Prime Minister?

Jim It seems to be necessary, Bernard. Government is seldom about right or wrong. It's about choosing the lesser evil.

Bernard (*stubborn*) It *can* be about right or wrong.

Jim Are you sure you're in the right job? I can always arrange a transfer, you know. Lambeth Palace, for instance.

Bernard You want to get rid of me?

Jim Not get rid of you, Bernard. A sideways move, find you a good home. Meanwhile, we have a crisis.

Bernard A moral crisis?

Jim A *survival* crisis, which is much more serious. *And* a moral crisis. I have to survive this weekend and stay in office. If I'm not, I can't do the things that the people elected me to do, the Health Service, schools and all that crap. I have a moral obligation to do whatever is necessary to stay in power.

Bernard I'm not sure that the end justifies the means. Look where that philosophy leads: Stalin wanted all the farms in the Ukraine collectivised. He thought there'd be more food. The peasant farmers opposed him, so he ordered all five million of them to be killed.

Jim Actually, if you kill five million people there *is* more food.

Bernard Does that make it right?

Jim Depends on whether or not you're one of the five million.

Claire re-enters.

Where did you go?

Claire I heard a dog bark out there. I recognised it.
It belongs to the cook. The illegal immigrant cook,
remember?

Jim Oh! I forgot about the cook! What are we doing
about that?!

Bernard Claire, really! We have more pressing matters
tonight.

Claire That was the cook's daughter out there, walking
the dog. Her sixteen-year-old daughter.

Jim and Bernard stare at her, stunned.

Jim And you're suggesting . . .?

Claire Yes. She looks about twelve.

Jim Does she?

Claire She's not a virgin. She's had sex. More than once.

Bernard How on earth do you know?

Claire I asked her.

Bernard And she just . . . told you?

Claire nods.

Jim But . . . but . . . but . . .

Claire An illegal immigrant. Exactly what you wanted.

Jim But the daughter of a member of our staff here . . .
Did you tell her what we want her to do?

Claire I sort of hinted at it.

Jim What precisely did you hint?

Bernard A hint can't be precise, Prime Minister, because by definition –

Jim Bernard!

Claire Sex with a very rich and powerful man. She seems interested.

Jim It's for Britain, right? It's the right thing to do, right?

Claire Jim, you were the one who said it would be patriotic. 'An act of the greatest nobility,' you said. Just let her lie back and think of England.

Jim She's a foreigner, it can't be patriotic for her.

Claire It will be when her papers come through. You're giving her a chance to serve her new country.

Bernard An act of retrospective patriotism?

Jim Shut up, Bernard! Claire, the answer is . . . no. Not *her*. I just can't go through with it.

Claire Okay.

She shrugs and turns to go.

Bernard Claire! Wait! What if the girl tells her mother?

Claire I took care of that. I asked her if she'd ever heard of the Detention Centre at Harmondsworth.

Bernard Had she?

Claire Of course, it's notorious. Like asking if she'd heard of Abu Ghraib. I told her 'If you ever tell anyone about this, including your mother, that's where you'll end up.' I couldn't threaten anything worse. I'll go and tell the girl it's off for tonight.

Claire exits to the garden.
Jim's anxiety has been building. It is reaching a high level.

82

Jim Phone the Home Secretary. Get citizenship for the cook.

Bernard Why?

Jim Because . . . What if she *does* tell her mother?

Bernard Hopefully, she won't.

Jim But if she does? How would the mother react?

Bernard Probably . . . not awfully well. How would you react if you were her mother?

Jim You know . . . I wonder if I might be pleased. It would give me the leverage to get a work permit.

Bernard stares at him for a moment.

Bernard How many drinks have you had, Prime Minister?

Jim Not many. Why?

Claire comes in from the garden.

Claire Okay. She's gone.

Jim Thank God!

Bernard To get her a work permit she needs to have special skills.

Jim She makes great dumplings . . . I don't bloody care! Phone the Home Secretary now!

Bernard (*glances at his watch*) Now?

Jim Yes, NOW, DAMMIT!

Bernard crosses to phone, and dials.

Bernard Ah, hello. Um – Sorry to wake you, Home Secretary . . . Oh, you're just having a nightcap? Good. The PM asked me to call you about the cook at Chequers . . . The cook . . . I know it's nearly midnight, but we've found out she's an illegal immigrant, and he wants her to be given a UK visa immediately . . . I *think*, because the PM likes her dumplings . . . No, that's not a sexist remark, Home Secretary . . . I see, thanks. (*Rings off.*) So sorry, Prime Minister, I think the Home Secretary's had a few, it's never any use trying to talk to her after six p.m.

Claire Do you think we'd better let the Ambassador know that we can't get Aitikeev a girl?

Jim Yes. Go and get him.

> *Bernard exits.*
> *The phone rings. Jim backs away from it in horror.*

Claire! Get the phone!

> *She answers it.*

Claire Yes? . . . Who? . . . Oh yes. We all *loved* your goulash and dumplings this evening . . . Yes . . . Yes . . . (*Writing down the phone number.*) I'll phone you back.

> *She hangs up.*

The cook's daughter has talked to her mother.

Jim Already?

Claire The cook wants to talk to you, Jim.

> *They stare at each other, paralysed by indecision. The phone rings again.*

Jim I'm not answering it. You get it!

Claire I don't know what to say!

Jim Just get it!

> *Bernard enters.*

Bernard The Ambassador's coming.

He sees their catatonic state, and answers the phone. Humphrey follows Bernard into the room a few moments later.

Yes? . . . Yes? . . . My God! . . . And where did you get this? . . . Of course I deny it. Yes. There is absolutely no foundation at all for that story . . . Of course you can't quote me, I'm not going dignify that rubbish with a comment.

He hangs up. Jim and Claire are anxiously staring at him.

It seems that the cook has talked to the *Daily Mail*.

Humphrey What about?

Claire She only just phoned here.

Bernard Well, she just phoned there too.

Jim Oh – my – God!

Humphrey What's the problem?

They are all ignoring him.

Claire Can we buy them off with a promise of special access? Some future diplomatic or policy scoop for them alone?

Jim Course not, it's a newspaper. They're interested in sex, not government.

Claire Jim, I think you'd better talk to the cook? We have to stop it going any further.

Humphrey Stop *what* going any further?

Jim I can't possibly.

Claire She was very insistent.

Jim I don't talk to ordinary people unless there's an election going on.

Claire If you don't, goodness knows what she'll –

Jim Phone her back and ask her just what the hell she wants!

Claire gives Bernard the phone number. Bernard takes a deep breath, then dials.

Humphrey What is all this *about*?

Bernard Yes, it's the Prime Minister's Principal Private Secretary here. Unfortunately he is too busy to talk to you, so can you please tell me what you want? . . . I see . . . I see . . . I see . . .

With each 'I see' his voice gets gloomier and gloomier.

I see.

He hangs up.

She's discovered the newspapers will give her cash . . . if her daughter will tell what happened tonight in her own words.

Humphrey Which are . . . ?

Bernard Um . . . that some woman approached her in the garden and asked her daughter to have sex . . . with you, Prime Minister.

Jim With *me*?!

Humphrey Is that true?

Jim No, of course it's not!!

Bernard I'm just telling you what she . . .

Jim (*grabs Bernard by the lapels*) It's an outrageous lie!

Bernard I'm just the messenger! (*Points at Claire.*) It was her idea! I knew it would be disastrous.

Claire What does she want?

Bernard Whaddya think? Money!

Bernard straightens his jacket and tie.

Humphrey Prime Minister – I think I understand what's been going on and I have an idea. I may know how to deal with this? May I?

Jim (*heartfelt*) Yes! Please!

Humphrey leaves the room, shutting the door firmly behind him – just short of a slam. Bernard sits in a corner, scowling at Claire, and sulks.

Claire We have to stop this going public.

Bernard (*bitter*) Brilliant! Got any more bright ideas?

Jim is nearly at the end of his tether. Claire is thinking.

Claire Look. As far as the *Mail* knows, it could be a scam. If we deny it and they still run the story we slap a libel writ on them and clean up financially. And deport her.

Jim is quietly chewing his knuckles in panic.

Jim Yes, she's not important in the great scheme of things.

Bernard Who is?

Jim Well – I am, actually. What's our story going to be, when the press talk to us?

Claire We say we can't talk about it. National security.

Jim How do we describe procuring sex with the cook's daughter as national security?

Claire We don't talk about that!

Jim That's what the papers will want to talk about!

Claire For God's sake, Jim! You don't give journalists what they want, it only encourages them!

Jim (*abject terror*) Oh my God! Oh my God! Oh my God! What do we do, we can't ignore the facts.

Bernard If you can't ignore the facts, Prime Minister, you have no business being in government.

Humphrey enters, smiling.

Humphrey It's done. The cook and her daughter were upstairs in their accommodation. At your request the Diplomatic Protection Group has taken them into protective custody and is turning them over to the Ministry of Defence Police.

Jim My request?!

Humphrey Under the Prevention of Terrorism Act and Article 10 of the Anti-Terror, Crime and Security Act, the MoD Police have complete police jurisdiction over the entire UK. They have the power to arrest, detain and then place a control order upon anyone at all.

Jim What's a control order?

Humphrey House arrest, for instance. Plus no access to mobile phones, the internet or the media – wherever they believe that lives may be saved or injuries prevented by so doing. Lasts for up to a year.

Jim Fine. Impose a control order.

Humphrey The Home Secretary has to do that.

Jim Oh, not her!

Humphrey With the approval of the High Court.

Jim Who says?

Humphrey The European Convention on Human Rights.

Jim Bloody Europe again! Taking away our rights.

Bernard Well, actually, Prime Minister, taking away your rights but increasing everybody else's.

Jim So they're entitled to a trial?

Humphrey Yes but, broadly speaking, a trial is subject to review – which can be held in secret and the evidence against them withheld from them and their lawyers.

Jim Oh, that's good! But the Home Secretary has to square it with a court?

Claire And the British people.

Humphrey They're not relevant. They don't speak for anyone.

Claire Except themselves.

Jim How can we give any weight to their opinions? They're not in full possession of the facts.

Claire Only because we don't tell them.

Jim None of their damn business.

Humphrey The British public don't need to know, dear lady.

Jim They don't *want* to know. Look at the newspapers they read.

Claire But it looks like we have to make a deal with the Home Secretary.

Bernard I can try to get her Private Secretary to bounce it past her one evening when she's had a few.

Jim And if that doesn't work?

Humphrey Tell her you have to make a list of suggestions for Companion of Honour. There's a vacancy coming up.

Jim Brilliant! But – it has to be a promise to get her cooperation.

Humphrey Think of it as a political promise, Prime Minister. Then you won't have to keep it.

Jim Okay, fine.

Humphrey At this point, the MoD Police only need an allegation: are you prepared to state that they are, in fact, terrorists?

Jim I am prepared to state the following. Categorically. Um . . . I . . . um . . .

Bernard Prime Minister, I think you are prepared to state to the police that both the cook and her daughter are in possession of information that, if it were known, could lead to a rapid escalation of violence leading to the loss of thousands more lives in the ongoing war.

Jim Yes I am. (*Relieved.*) That's actually true! Make a note of what you just said.

Bernard does. There's a knock on the door. Humphrey gets there and opens it. The Ambassador is standing there.

Humphrey Freddie. Is the Prime Minister expecting . . .?

Bernard Yes he is. Come in please, Your Excellency. (*To Jim.*) The Kumranistan Ambassador, Prime Minister.

Jim Yes, come in.

Ambassador Thank you, Prime Minister.

Humphrey exits, closing the door.

Jim I'm not going to beat about the bush. I'm afraid you'll have to tell Mr Aitikeev that we were unable to find a suitable . . . candidate.

Ambassador He's guessed that by now, Prime Minister. *I'm* afraid that half an hour ago, he informed our President that he does not find you sympathetic to our national aspirations. The pipeline deal is, I'm afraid, off.

Jim Oh? Is it? Then tell your Mr Aitikeev that if he withdraws from this pipeline agreement, all those weapons systems we sold you will be cancelled forthwith.

Ambassador But we have them already, Prime Minister.

Jim We'll stop supplying the spare parts. They'll be useless within months. Full of sand. Probably are already.

Ambassador It won't matter, Prime Minister. We are making a new weapons agreement with the Russians.

Jim You are? Then please inform Mr Aitikeev that Great Britain is breaking off diplomatic relations with your country.

Ambassador (*shocked*) Are you serious?

Jim I am. I'm giving you forty-eight hours to get to Heathrow Airport.

Ambassador What do you think I am? A snail?

He walks out.

Bernard Was that wise, Prime Minister?

Jim I don't know and I no longer care!

Bernard sits.

Bernard I think I lost my moral compass tonight. I can tell you one thing: this incident will not be in my memoirs.

Claire Of course not. Memoirs are not the truth, they're the case for the defence.

Jim I think Humphrey's right. It's all over! (*A deep and heartfelt sigh.*) Bernard, tomorrow morning, arrange for me to see the Queen and offer my resignation.

Bernard I'm so sorry, Prime Minister.

Jim nods, hopelessly. There is a sad and awkward silence.
Suddenly, another huge flash of lightning and a thunderclap. The lights flicker and go out.

Jim Oh God!

As he speaks, Sir Humphrey enters, seen in majestic silhouette.

Humphrey No, Prime Minister, just me.

The lights flicker back on.

I have returned with the answer to all your problems: global warming!

Jim What?

Bernard He said 'global warming', Prime Mini—

Jim I heard what he said! What does he mean? (*To Humphrey.*) I thought you were against it.

Humphrey Everyone's against it, Prime Minister. I suddenly realised, that's the beauty of it! We can get a unanimous agreement with our European partners to do something about it.

Jim How can we do something about something that isn't happening?

Humphrey Much easier to solve an imaginary problem than a real one. If everyone thinks global warming's real, they'll all want to stop it. As long as it doesn't cost too much.

Jim Do you believe it's real?

Humphrey Do you?

Jim I don't know.

Humphrey Nor do I. Haven't the faintest idea. But it doesn't matter what we think. The question is, what do we do about it?

Jim If it isn't happening, what *can* we do about it?

Humphrey There's *so much* we can do: impose taxes, stiffen European rules about carbon emissions and rubbish disposal, make massive investments in wind turbines . . . we can agree, in fact, under your leadership, to save the world.

Jim I like that.

Claire But Russia, India, China, Brazil . . . they'll never cooperate.

Humphrey They won't have to. We simply ask them to agree to review their emissions policy.

Jim And will they?

Humphrey Of course. And they'll decide not to change it. Meanwhile you can talk about the future, look statesmanlike, and it will be fifty years before anybody can prove you were wrong.

Claire You can pick up green votes without losing your core voters . . .

Bernard And you can explain away anything you've said previously by saying the computer models were flawed . . .

Jim The voters will love me . . .

Claire (*warning*) You'll have more government expenditure.

Jim Yes, how would we pay for it? We're broke.

Humphrey Raise a special global-warming tax on fuel now. But phase in expenditure gradually, over the next fifty years . . .

Jim That would get us out of the hole now . . .

Claire *And* our allies . . .

Humphrey That's all we need.

Jim Everyone benefits. Conservation . . . reducing dependence on foreign oil . . . an excuse to abandon the pipeline . . .

Claire The Germans have a big green movement, they'll be pleased . . .

Bernard We can get the Frogs on board as long as they get more benefits than anyone else . . .

Jim Okay. My broadcast is Sunday morning. You've got today to get the conference to agree.

Humphrey That's not a problem. They'll be desperate to announce something when they get home on Monday. What we're offering is like the bag of sweeties you give kids to take home after a party.

Bernard There is one problem . . . Nothing will have actually been achieved.

Humphrey It will sound as though it has. And people will think it has.

Jim That's what matters.

Blackout.

*Jim is at his desk. A Union Jack and an EU flag are
displayed behind him.*

*Simon Chester, a BBC interviewer, is facing him across
the desk. There are cameras on them both.*

Perhaps the audience can see the output on monitors.

*Humphrey and Bernard are seated at the side,
watching on their own monitor. A helmeted Despatch
Rider with a package enters and stands next to Humphrey
and Bernard.*

Simon (*talks to camera*) So, to summarise, there is a
deepening financial crisis, division in the Cabinet, opinion
polls are at their lowest for seven years, government
borrowing at an all-time high and apparently no
agreement on what to do about it all at the Lancaster
House Conference. Today's papers are asking if Jim
Hacker's government can survive. I'm here in Chequers,
live with the Prime Minister. (*Turns to Jim.*) Can you
survive, Prime Minister?

Jim Of course. All governments go through difficult
patches –

Simon Yes, but this is more than just a difficult patch,
isn't it?

Jim It's a world problem, it obviously has repercussions
on the UK, but we . . .

Simon But it is worse here than anywhere else, isn't it?

*Humphrey taps the Despatch Rider on the shoulder.
The Despatch Rider walks into the shot and hands a
folder to Jim.*

Jim (*opens it*) Excuse me a second. I've been waiting
for this. I think you'll find this puts a very different

complexion on things. It is perhaps the most momentous document you'll ever see.

Now, out of Simon's view, the Despatch Rider takes off her helmet and we see that it is, in fact, Claire.

Simon May we know what it is?

Jim It's the final communiqué from the conference: a binding agreement on all members of the European Union to devote unprecedented sums to the battle against global warming. You saw the latest IPCC report? That the situation is not only far more serious than we thought but also deteriorating far more quickly.

Simon Yes, that was one of the things I was coming to, but if we could talk first about the level of debt –

Jim I obviously haven't made myself clear. I'm not talking about day-to-day issues, I'm talking about the survival of life on this planet. I do realise that you have to try and score your political points. That's your job. But the new findings on global warming make all other issues insignificant.

Simon You can't call our debt level insignificant –

Jim Look, Simon, *you* can chase all the little preoccupations of daily journalism. As Prime Minister, I have to look to the future of our country and the world. Not tomorrow's headlines but ten, twenty, fifty years ahead. A heavy responsibility. This document is so momentous. It commits Europe to an investment of five trillion euros to stop global warming.

Simon How can we possibly afford to spend that sum of money?

Jim We can't afford not to.

Simon But if the money's not there –

Jim We are faced with a catastrophic rise in sea levels. Torrential storms. Melting ice caps. Widespread hunger. Mass migrations.

Simon Are you sure?

Jim Computer models don't lie. They have no ulterior motive.

Simon But five trillion euros . . .

Jim Over time. In the early years it will be less, of course. We have much research to do on – (*cribs from folder*) carbon sequestration plants, new fast-breeder reactors, biofuels . . .

Simon Even so, surely taxes will have to go up. People won't like –

Jim Simon, people aren't as selfish as you think they are. They are worried about their children, their grandchildren, the future of mankind. If it means doing without a gas-guzzler or a fourth plasma TV set, that's a sacrifice most people are willing to make.

Simon Prime Minister, I did want to talk to you about Cabinet divisions –

Jim There's no Cabinet division on the survival of our species or the future of life on this planet. They will support the prospect of all this investment in twenty years' time.

Simon They won't be in office then.

Jim I think that's an unworthy remark. Are you saying that a government can't make commitments beyond the immediate future?

Simon No, but twenty years!

Jim We are looking at a historic consensus. The agreement of every single country in the European Union. It will stand alongside Magna Carta and the American Declaration of Independence.

Simon I'm afraid that time is getting a little short . . .

Jim (*ignoring him*) And future generations will look back and thank us for putting their future above our own narrow, selfish, short-term interests.

Simon Okay. To move on quickly –

Jim And if I might just strike a personal note, I would like to say how humble it makes me to think that I, as President of – the Commission was able to bring about this historic agreement which, quite frankly, transcends any achievement of any post-war government. It is, as I say, humbling. Deeply humbling.

Simon Thank you, Prime Minister. (*To camera.*) And there we have to leave it. Until next week, goodbye.

> *The screens go blank. Applause from Humphrey, Bernard and Claire.*

Jim Well, Simon, you certainly know how to do a tough interview.

Simon Thank you, Prime Minister.

> *He walks out, a defeated man.*

Humphrey Magnificent, Prime Minister.

Claire I think you got away with it, Jim. But the Cabinet will have been pretty surprised, we'll have to square them fast. Also, I've been in touch with some press agents . . .

Jim Bob Geldof?

Claire Can't reach him, but we're waiting to hear from Bono.

Jim Okay.

Claire And I just got a text from Angelina Jolie and Brad Pitt! They will endorse this!

Jim is triumphant, ecstatic.

Jim That's it! That's all we need! Cabinet will never go against that. I'm back.

Bernard Claire, give me their contact details and I'll get them to a dinner at Number Ten.

Claire One more thing, Prime Minister. I do think that after that interview you need to announce some pretty impressive action to make it look as though you're serious.

Jim An initiative?

Humphrey Yes.

Jim A working party?

Claire A bit lightweight.

Jim Task force?

Claire Not sure.

Jim Have we got enough in the kitty?

Bernard It could be one of those initiatives which you announce but never actually spend the money . . .

Claire Like the one on child poverty.

Jim Maybe it should be a government committee?

Humphrey What about a Royal Commission?

Jim That's more like it. It won't report for three years. And if we put the right people on it they won't agree about anything important. Right, a Royal Commission.

Claire No, hold on. That makes it sound as if we think it's important but not urgent.

Jim So what do you suggest?

Humphrey What about a Global-Warming Czar?

Jim Fine. Will that do it?

Humphrey I think it would need a bit more than that, Prime Minister.

Jim Such as?

Humphrey It will mean announcing quite a big unit. And an impressive salary for the Czar. To show how much importance you place upon the appointment.

Jim No problem. Who should it be?

Humphrey It mustn't be a political figure. Too divisive. Someone impartial. Someone who knows how to operate the levers of power. Engage the gears of the Whitehall machine. Drive the engine of government.

Jim That's quite a tall order. Anyone got any ideas? (*Stares at Humphrey.*) Humphrey! Could you . . .?

Humphrey Yes, Prime Minister.

Blackout.

Curtain.